"Matthew Boedy reveals in painstaking detail . . . how the seven mountains mandate quietly became the 'dominant religious framework among American Christians' after Donald Trump's election facilitated its spread from evangelical fringes to the White House, powerful financial backers, and supporters emboldened by 'divine urgency' to enact 'God's plan.' It's a sobering assessment of the evolution of Christian nationalism."

—*PUBLISHERS WEEKLY*

"One of the most important books to come out this year, *The Seven Mountains Mandate* masterfully charts the current struggle for the American soul. Through his lucid writing and meticulous research, Boedy details the right-wing crusade to impose Christian control over government, family, religion, education, business, media, and entertainment. Is that possible? In 2024, the movement behind the mandate, decades in the making, overcame theological and denominational differences to help elect President Donald Trump. Now, with the White House on their side, activists like Charlie Kirk on the march, and Fox News creating their own reality, supporters of the seven mountain mandate are on their way to, as Boedy fears, Christianizing America and destroying democracy. If you want to understand the who, what, why, when, where, and how of white Christian nationalism, *The Seven Mountains Mandate* is where to start."

—**DIANE WINSTON**, Knight Chair in Media and Religion, Annenberg School for Communication and Journalism, University of Southern California

"Boedy offers a vital and incisive account of how dominionist ideology has saturated the political imagination of much of American evangelicalism. As a pastor who has spent years navigating the fallout of Christian nationalism in my congregation and community, I'm deeply grateful for Boedy's clarity, scholarship, and moral courage. This book is a needed resource for those seeking to faithfully resist the powers that would co-opt the way of Jesus for political domination."

—**CALEB E. CAMPBELL**, author of *Disarming Leviathan: Loving Your Christian Nationalist Neighbor*

"We cannot change where we're going without knowing where we've been, which is why Boedy's work in *The Seven Mountains Mandate* is so vitally important. With expertise and candor, Boedy illuminates the history of theocracy and antidemocracy in this country that has too often hidden underneath a thin veneer of Christian rhetoric. This book is especially important as we attempt to navigate our way through Trump's second administration and push back against the onslaught of Christian nationalism."

—**ZACH W. LAMBERT**, pastor of Restore Church in Austin, Texas, and author of *Better Ways to Read the Bible: Transforming a Weapon of Harm into a Tool of Healing*

"Gifted at translating the seven mountains mandate into its political and social realities, Boedy illustrates how this transformative doctrine affects the lives of believers and nonbelievers alike."

—**ELLE HARDY**, journalist and author of *Beyond Belief: How Pentecostal Christianity Is Taking Over the World*

"Boedy, a professor of rhetoric at the University of North Georgia, provides a succinct, readable overview of 7MM [the seven mountains mandate] and . . . highlighting the role of Charlie Kirk, founder and president of Turning Point USA (TPUSA)—the nation's preeminent conservative youth organization—in making 7MM 'the central organizing element of the Trump era' and thereby bringing us to 'the precipice of the destruction of our democracy.'"

—*SPECTRUM MAGAZINE*

The Seven Mountains Mandate

The Seven Mountains Mandate is ideal for discussing with others. Visit **www.wjkbooks.com/SevenMountains** to access free resources, including a book club guide, an eight-session guide for using the book in adult group study at your church or organization, and videos from the author that engage each of the mountains in the seven mountains mandate.

The Seven Mountains Mandate

*Exposing the Dangerous Plan
to Christianize America
and Destroy Democracy*

MATTHEW BOEDY

© 2025 Matthew Boedy

First edition
Published by Westminster John Knox Press
Louisville, Kentucky

25 26 27 28 29 30 31 32 33 34—10 9 8 7 6 5 4 3 2

All rights reserved. No part of this book may be reproduced or transmitted in any form or by any means, electronic or mechanical, including photocopying, recording, or by any information storage or retrieval system, without permission in writing from the publisher. For information, address Westminster John Knox Press, 100 Witherspoon Street, Louisville, Kentucky 40202-1396. Or contact us online at www.wjkbooks.com.

Unless otherwise indicated, Scripture quotations are from *The Holy Bible, New International Version.* Copyright © 1973, 1978, 1984, 2011 by Biblica, Inc.® Used by permission. All rights reserved worldwide.

Book design by Sharon Adams
Cover design by Erika Lundbom

Library of Congress Cataloging-in-Publication Data

Names: Boedy, Matthew Neal author
Title: The seven mountains mandate : exposing the dangerous plan to
   Christianize America and destroy democracy / Matthew Boedy.
Description: First edition. | Louisville, Kentucky : Westminster John Knox
   Press, [2025] | Includes bibliographical references and index. |
   Summary: "Uncovers the fruition of Project 2025 policies being enacted
   with Trump's return to office, discussing what has motivated the key
   players in this movement and the unprecedented role of Charlie Kirk,
   founder of Turning Point USA, who was the first to connect Trump to the
   Seven Mountains Movement"-- Provided by publisher.
Identifiers: LCCN 2025024646 (print) | LCCN 2025024647 (ebook) | ISBN
   9780664269210 hardback | ISBN 9781646984350 ebook
Subjects: LCSH: Christianity and politics--United States--History--21st
   century | Democracy--United States--History--21st century |
   Nationalism--United States--History--21st century |
   Nationalism--Religious aspects--Christianity | Kirk, Charlie | Trump,
   Donald, 1946---Influence
Classification: LCC BR516 .B64 2025 (print) | LCC BR516 (ebook)
LC record available at https://lccn.loc.gov/2025024646
LC ebook record available at https://lccn.loc.gov/2025024647

PRINTED IN THE UNITED STATES OF AMERICA

∞ The paper used in this publication meets the minimum requirements of the American National Standard for Information Sciences—Permanence of Paper for Printed Library Materials, ANSI Z39.48-1992.

Most Westminster John Knox Press books are available at special quantity discounts when purchased in bulk by corporations, organizations, and special-interest groups. For more information, please e-mail SpecialSales@wjkbooks.com.

**Key Dates in the Development of the
Seven Mountains Mandate Movement**

1973   **R. J. Rushdoony**, Calvinist theologian known as the father of Christian Reconstructionism, publishes *The Institutes of Biblical Law*, focused on applying the Ten Commandments to institutions such as the family, education, the marketplace, and other arenas of our modern social order.

1975   **Bill Bright**, founder of Campus Crusade for Christ, and **Loren Cunningham**, founder of Youth with a Mission, meet up in Colorado and share that they've each received a vision regarding seven areas or spheres of cultural influence. **Francis Schaeffer**, founder of L'Abri communities, is also associated with the 1975 vision, though he was not present in Colorado.

1981   **C. Peter Wagner,** Fuller Seminary professor and father of the New Apostolic Reformation, publishes *Church Growth and the Whole Gospel: A Biblical Mandate*, asserting that Christians are charged with Christianizing society's institutions.

1989   **John Dawson**, a former staffer with Cunningham's Youth with a Mission, publishes *Taking Our Cities for God*, a guide to spiritual mapping that emphasizes six spheres of influence in cities (media being the seventh).

2000   **Lance Wallnau**, enterprising pastor, learns about the seven spheres from Cunningham. He is introduced to Wagner's network of apostles in 2001 and soon popularizes "mountains" as the predominant metaphor for the seven spheres of society.

2008   **Wagner** publishes *Dominion! How Kingdom Action Can Change the World*, endorsing Cunningham and Wallnau's approach to installing Christian leaders atop the seven mountains of society.

2012   **Charlie Kirk** founds Turning Point USA the summer after his high school graduation, following publicity he gained writing a piece for Breitbart accusing teachers and textbook creators of liberal indoctrination.

2019   **Rob McCoy**, California megachurch pastor and local officeholder, introduces Kirk to the seven mountains mandate movement.

2020   **Kirk** speaks at the Conservative Political Action Conference and says of Donald Trump, "Finally, we have a president who understands the seven mountains of cultural influence."

2024   On the eve of Trump's second election, the *Atlantic* calls Kirk "the right's new kingmaker."

Contents

Preface	ix
Introduction: The Story of the Mountains	1
1. God's 1776 Project: The Mountain of Education	21
2. Counselor to the King: The Mountain of Government	43
3. Biblical Citizenship: The Mountain of Religion	59
4. The Masculine Heart and the Feminine Mystique: The Mountain of Family	77
5. Marketplace Apostles in God's Economy: The Mountain of Business	97
6. What's Really Happening: The Mountain of Media	113
7. The Left Can't Meme: The Mountain of Entertainment	127
Afterword	145
Acknowledgments	147
Notes	149
Index	173

Preface

Watching the first inauguration of Donald Trump was heartbreaking enough. A second inauguration means that by the time you read this, the worst predictions of his second term may already be coming true.

Many of those predictions came from a plan called Project 2025, which you may have heard about during the campaign and in the months following. It is a collection of actions Trump's allies wanted the new president to undertake within the first 180 days of his administration. Many of those actions became Trump's executive orders signed in his first week. Implementing fully the wide-ranging playbook would eliminate some cabinet-level agencies, slash the power of others, and erode the civil rights of many Americans. Supporters of Project 2025—which include the organization at the heart of this book—want to erase what they see as a decades-long political and social weaponization of government against conservative values.

But that massive change in government is not the only goal for the people and organizations involved in the seven mountains mandate movement. Government is just one of seven "mountains" of culture the movement wants to radically change. That more expansive strategy is grounded in an ideology called Christian nationalism. Who is included in that label, what they believe, and how deep those beliefs go was analyzed in depth throughout the 2024 campaign.

This book won't repeat that debate. What this book will do is lay out the movement's sweeping plan to Christianize America that now has its champion controlling the levers of government. But the plan long predates Trump. Since the 1970s it has been gaining ground within evangelical churches, schools, and media. And while not secret, advocates of the plan have become so despondent for total cultural power that if they lose one mountain, they revolt. See the 2021 insurrection.

Now that Trump has won again, advocates of the seven mountains mandate have success for all the mountains within reach. But Trump isn't the only reason for that. Much of the success can be linked to a conservative youth political outreach group started in a small garage in Illinois by a teen more than ten years ago. Now in his thirties and armed with boundless political influence, this man has become the mandate's heir.

Charlie Kirk, founder and president of Turning Point USA, has continued to inflame the fear of anti-Christian persecution that gave birth to the seven mountains mandate. But he isn't just repeating decades of talking points that have gained him followers and financial success. He has acted in significant ways to cement the seven mountains mandate as the central organizing element of the Trump era. During the Biden administration, this meant fighting what the movement considered a corrupt regime conspiring against God and his vision for America. Now it means policy and laws that keep the God of evangelicalism the ruler not merely of our politics but of all other cultural, economic, and business arenas. Through millions of dollars and by the power of its millions of followers, Turning Point has the nation standing on the precipice of the destruction of our democracy.

More than thirty years ago, when the seven mountains mandate movement was still in its infancy, one of the first observers of the plan asked a disturbing question about its sweeping claims and outsized goal to Christianize America. Sociologist Sara Diamond wrote that the plan may sound hopelessly unrealistic, but its early success meant we had to ask at what cost more success would come.

Now a generation later, those costs have grown exponentially. The mandate movement has the most autocratic president in American history supporting it at every step. Supporters of the mandate like Kirk now stand ready to use and abuse the levers of democratic power to deliver on all the movement has been promising. How they are planning to do so is what this book is about.

Introduction

The Story of the Mountains

The plan to Christianize America began fifty years ago with a vision from God.

Or so the legend goes.

Bill Bright, the founder of a college campus evangelism organization, had just landed in Colorado in August 1975 to participate in an event in Boulder. But something planted deep in his spirit had made Bright desperate to talk to Loren Cunningham, a founder of another youth-oriented evangelism organization, who was on vacation in Colorado.

The vision from God that Bright had brought for Cunningham was a typed list of seven influential areas of culture. If Christians could win these seven areas for Christ, Bright said, the nation could be set right and return to its biblical origins. It would take a massive spiritual war, but ending the demonic control of these areas would have immense impact for the kingdom of God.

The problem was that God had placed Cunningham on a mountaintop near Durango on the other side of the state with no way to communicate. The man who had picked up Bright at the airport said he could get the two together. Someone got through to a ranger station in Durango, and then from there someone on horseback found Cunningham's remote location. That man took Cunningham to a borrowed plane, which flew Cunningham to meet the man who had that urgent message from God. What Bright didn't know was that God had given Cunningham the same list, though his was sketched out on a legal pad. The two friends presented their lists to each other simultaneously. Cunningham later wrote, "Amazing coincidences like this happen all the time when Christians listen to the still, small voice of the Holy Spirit."[1]

Over the years, the story of that 1975 meeting has been told many ways, accepted not merely as gospel but a divine endorsement of the list Bright and Cunningham created. Whatever the truth of the meeting, the list has become powerful spiritual lore passed down from one generation to another in the movement born from it. That movement is intent on destroying democracy by taking dominion in these seven institutions: education, family, religion, government, business, media, and entertainment.[2] Over the decades, many have made their mark on the list by envisioning different labels for it. While Bright and Cunningham spoke of areas of influence, others have called them gates, pillars, channels, and—most commonly among the movement's supporters today—mountains. The preferred metaphor evolved over time, but the purpose of the list has remained the same: bring the kingdom of God to America by conquering each of these cultural domains.

The story of the seven mountains movement told in this book is the story of those who inspired and shaped that 1975 list. It's also about how the list has come to dominate American political life in the twenty-first century without most Americans even having heard about it. This insidious victory is the work of a new generation of believers who have pushed it with more and more aggression, pushing us closer and closer to violence, threatening our society through their claim to divine urgency. In short, this is the story of how the list became a mandate.

The spiritual energy behind this mandate pushed the list into the White House with the 2016 election of Donald Trump. From there the movement exploded beyond the fringes of charismatic evangelicalism into larger institutions, influencers, and financial backers. To a handful of experts who have followed the movement for years, it was no surprise its supporters turned violent when the 2020 election didn't go the way they wanted—the way they say God wanted. This is where the movement has been headed. Yet even more frighteningly, since the 2021 insurrection at the Capitol, more Americans seemingly want what the seven mountains movement wants. A June 2023 survey of two thousand Americans estimated that about 30 percent "are open to" ideas associated with the seven mountains movement such as "U.S. culture is 'fundamentally Christian'" and "Christian values should be 'solely and explicitly endorsed by the government.'" Another 2023 survey found a similar percentage of Americans either adhering to or sympathetic to those ideals.[3] A second Trump administration only reinforces that.

Of course, many of the Americans in those polls are the demographic most supportive of the mandate: evangelicals. A 2024 survey showed that strong majorities of evangelicals agree broadly with the goals of the seven mountains movement. About 55 percent of evangelicals specifically agreed that "God wants Christians to stand atop the Seven Mountains of society." The survey also showed that the percentage of Christian Americans who believed in the mandate increased from just under 30 percent to 41 percent in one year.[4] The surveyors noted that "what not long ago seemed to be a marginal set of beliefs has become a dominant religious framework among American Christians."[5]

The seven mountains movement has been adopted across the religious right even by leaders who may not share its theology, because their followers are being motivated by the mandate. For example, the 2022 National Day of Prayer guide from the Southern Baptist Convention—the nation's largest Protestant denomination and traditionally one devoted to religious liberty for all—asked its congregants to pray for the "seven centers of influence."[6] Beyond religion, the seven mountains movement has become so accepted in American society that its supporters from all levels of government, from Congress to school boards, have publicly named themselves as supporters. One expert said in 2021 that it is "a heartbeat away from everything that happens in the Republican Party."[7]

The seven mountains movement is an all-encompassing strategy of a larger ideology known as Christian nationalism. The 2021 insurrection made a wider swath of Americans aware of the antidemocratic violence within that ideology. Those violent desires have not faded even after hundreds of convictions and long prison sentences for some involved in the insurrection. The mass pardons for all involved from President Trump in his first week in office were not only a campaign promise kept but an explicit approval of those desires. It might then come as no surprise that a 2024 survey showed a majority of Christian nationalists would support a leader who is "willing to break some rules." About a third of those same people support "violence in order to save our country or to ensure that the rightful leader takes office." More than 80 percent agree that "the final battle between good and evil is upon us."[8]

After two election seasons where it was featured prominently, Christian nationalism continues to divide America. A poll of twenty-two thousand Americans in 2024 showed that "nearly four in ten residents of red states are Christian nationalists," and this "is nearly twice the proportion of blue state residents who are Christian nationalists." States with the highest levels of support for Christian nationalism range geographically from North Dakota to Louisiana.[9] Christian nationalism rests on the idea of restoring "the idea that Christian people should be privileged in the United States in some way—economically, socially, politically," according to religion scholar Bradley Onishi. "And that privilege is a result of the country being founded by and for Christians."[10] That founding mythology pushes many advocates of the seven mountains movement to demand that only Christians will have full voting rights in a nation run by the mandate.

The Heir to the List

Since the 2021 insurrection, many scholars and media outlets have brought new attention to Christian nationalism. Many examples in the expanding genre of books about the ideology have ended with warnings about the future. That future has appeared. The seven mountains movement's fathers like Bright have long since died (Cunningham died in 2023 in his nineties), and their heirs are well into senior citizen status. But just a few years ago a new heir was brought into the fold. This occurred in 2020 when a tall, thin, and well-dressed millennial in February walked onto the stage at the powerful Conservative Political Action Conference and announced to the nation that for the first time in its history it had a president who "understands the seven mountains of cultural influence."[11]

That heir is Charlie Kirk, founder of Turning Point USA. Kirk emerged in this role because he has deep pockets and millions of followers. In the last five years he has remade his national political organization to conquer the seven mountains. His success forces those previous warnings about Christian nationalism into a different, more alarming perspective. Kirk requires a recalibration because of what he brings to the movement and what he has already accomplished. He and Turning Point have brought the seven mountains movement as close to success as it has even been.

Kirk began Turning Point in the summer of 2012, just after graduating high school. His origin story about indoctrination in his high school had gone viral that April on the leading conservative news site, Breitbart, and Kirk quickly became a Fox News darling, got funding from major conservative backers, and launched his conservative youth outreach program from his garage in a Chicago suburb. Kirk built Turning Point by hosting debate-style events on college quads where he challenged shy conservatives to boldly believe and taunted liberal students with rhetorical fights he never seemed to lose. Kirk went all in on Trump in 2016, and his summits for students headlined by political celebrities ballooned into all-age affairs, with Trump often a guest. The organization's budgets exploded year after year. Since 2016 Turning Point has raised roughly a quarter-billion dollars.[12]

Now married and in his thirties with two kids, Kirk is a fast-talking radio host and social media provocateur who operates from Turning Point's sprawling campus in Phoenix, Arizona. You might call him a new Rush Limbaugh. (The famous conservative radio host complimented Kirk in 2018 and suggested that Kirk was "running the White House." Kirk continues to play that clip at the beginning of every episode of his radio program, which replaced Limbaugh in many markets after the icon's death.) But Kirk is much more than a leading voice in conservative politics. He has made Turning Point into the indispensable organization for the seven mountains movement. In 2021 Kirk pitched to investors a plan for "seven core outreach programs" that mirror the 1975 list. The plan painted a dire picture of America, playing off Turning Point's history attacking higher education, saying the "localized tumor of campus extremism has metastasized" and now threatens "the very life of our country." It blamed "secular elitists" for funding the left's "long march through the institutions of our society."[13]

That phrase about institutions was originally coined in the sixties by socialist countercultural writers. Turning Point has repurposed it for its goal of Christianizing America. But evangelism is not the central strategy for Turning Point and the larger movement it leads. The mandate movement operates as a minority movement. It's not counting on mass conversions. In fact, those like Kirk who want to expand Christian privilege are a shrinking minority. This status makes it a threat to democracy, but not just to the idea of majority rule. The seven mountains movement is a threat to the religious pluralism American democracy was built on.

This minority sees itself as God's chosen rulers. Many of them think reformation comes before revival, that political and social victories should lead spiritual ones. This is why so many in the seven mountains movement agree with the ideas that the church should have veto power over legislation.[14] Kirk understands the mandate movement's history, its link to Christian nationalism, and the waves of criticism and warnings since the insurrection. In response, he has recalibrated the movement. This is most obvious in how he speaks about the movement's history—or, rather, doesn't speak about it. He doesn't approach at all the divine origins of the movement itself. And he has only referred to the plan for the seven mountains publicly once—at that 2020 CPAC event. A Turning Point spokesman told NBC News in June 2024 that "Charlie probably couldn't tell you what the seven mountains are."[15]

But Kirk doesn't hide the goal of the seven mountains movement. He admits he is a Christian and a nationalist and defends the claim that people like him want to use "state power" to put Christianity in government: "I always laugh at that presupposition. We're going to put things that are right and good and beautiful and true in government. Of course we are."[16] While that may be the goal of the seven mountains movement, Kirk and Turning Point have used lies and fear to advance the mandate. But it's more than rhetoric. As we shall see in the pages to follow, Kirk's actions already have begun to erase much of what makes America great.

Origins of the Movement

Whether God played a role in inspiring Cunningham and Bright's list, as legends often go, it's clear their ideas stem from a theological and social world that spans two continents across decades, a world that those who advocate for the seven mountains movement today want to re-create under a Christian banner.

Part of the immediate context to which Bright and others were responding was the end of the "long '60s," that era which culminated in the antiwar protests and shootings at Kent State and Jackson State. It included years of race-based violence and civil rights marches often led by younger leaders. Outside the political arena, the decade left the nation divided along many well-known cultural fault lines. The list is a response to all that we associate with that decade—from drugs to music to sex to crumbling moral standards. The list is an implicit call for a return to the decade prior.

The list is also a reversal from decades of nonengagement in the culture by Christian fundamentalism. Churches and pastors who followed this way of thinking separated from the wicked world and its evil culture but also went as far as to separate themselves from fellow Christians whom they thought were not theologically pure or too negatively impacted by culture. Fundamentalists as a sect were derided in movies such as the 1960 release *Inherit the Wind*, which dramatized the 1925 Scopes trial.

While American evangelicalism has roots in the '30s and often agreed theologically with fundamentalists, in the post–World War II era it as a movement sought new ways to engage culturally and politically in America. Those who were pursuing innovation in evangelism were sometimes labeled neo-evangelicals. In 2014 Steven Patrick Miller wrote that the '70s in particular "witnessed a boom in public evangelicalism," and evangelicals showed a "renewed conviction that faith deserves a prominent place in the 'public square.'" To make the case for a new engagement, when writing about the 1975 list Cunningham referred to Luke 19:13 in the King James Version: "Jesus told us to occupy until He came. It's not occupying the earth if we hole up in a religious enclave and let everyone outside our church walls rot away."[17]

Bright's organization, then known as Campus Crusade for Christ, and Cunningham's Youth with a Mission were a significant part of this larger change in American evangelicalism's stance toward the world. These organizations helped evangelical leaders see the next generation as essential to the future of the church and nation. That meant not shying away from the youth's changing culture. They were not the only ones. A few years before the Colorado vision, the National Association of Evangelicals called in 1970 for its member churches to "initiate a new relationship with their youth by listening to them, believing in them, responding to them and encouraging them."[18]

Two years later Bright and his organization (now known merely as CRU) helped to organize a five-day evangelical youth summit known as Explo '72. The conference drew more than 80,000 students (some estimates put the daily crowd at more than 100,000) to the Cotton Bowl stadium in Dallas in June 1972. Johnny Cash, among many others, performed. Billy Graham spoke. The conference was considered the epitome of the Jesus Movement, a self-labeled countercultural Christian youth movement that began in California. The "culture" they were countering was the original counterculture movement that brought America Woodstock, second-wave feminism, the sexual revolution, and other events and trends in the late '60s. The historian Benjamin J. Young has argued that Explo '72 "wasn't a mere revival. Instead, it was a generational hinge in the history of modern American evangelicalism."[19]

There were plenty of reasons, then, in the summer of 1975 why Cunningham was "praying and thinking about how we could turn the world around for Jesus."[20] He wrote that Satan's authority over the world needed to be deposed. This kind of spiritual war rhetoric was growing in some evangelical circles, and the strategies to meet the moment were changing. Evangelism remained important, but it also meant that the gospel should capture entire societies in a broader, institutional fashion, especially the most influential areas of culture. Cunningham immediately put the list of seven areas to use in his organization, sharing it as early as September 1975 with British Youth with a Mission staff.[21] In 1978 Cunningham started a missionary training center in Hawaii to equip the next generation of leaders in this cultural transformation. Well into the twenty-first century, the list has remained a part of the organization's training.

Both Bright and Cunningham had started their respective organizations based on visions of global evangelism. In 1956, Cunningham had seen waves crashing ashore on all the continents. Bright's vision occurred as he was studying in seminary in 1951. God showed the young businessman how he and his generation would be used to reach all people. Bright calculated he would succeed by the late '70s. This impending deadline of sorts by the time of his meeting with Cunningham had pushed Bright to become a leader in moving evangelicals toward a more overt relationship between politics and religion.

This meant amid the religious goals, Bright had a political agenda for Explo '72. That agenda was so obvious that he had tried to get President Richard Nixon to appear at the event. The year before the mountaintop vision with Cunningham, with the aid of millions from conservative business tycoons, Bright started a publishing house whose books encouraged evangelicals to get involved in politics. He used that publisher to push a national evangelism effort that aimed to have 50,000 churches expand their congregations in eighteen major cities. A pilot program in Atlanta began in 1975. But that plan was exposed for its political undertones by a 1976 profile in a more liberal evangelical publication.[22]

Those efforts were the seeds for what came to be known as the religious right. Bright and others helped push that growing movement from supporting noted evangelical Jimmy Carter to helping elect Ronald Reagan in 1980. They soured on Carter for many reasons, but one seemed to be his support for "secular humanism," which included feminism and other trends they perceived as threatening to American families. These ideologies were among the many intellectual diseases sickening America that led Cunningham to label his seven areas "mind molders." Such ideas secured the demonic grip on American culture.

Throughout the ensuing decades, Bright kept pushing Christian leaders, especially those who had influence due to their business success, to become public advocates for Christian culture. One acolyte of Bright's says he was challenged by Bright in 1996 to start a group for business leaders in Arizona to influence the culture. Nearly thirty years later that group has chapters across the nation and is grounded in the seven mountains.[23] Bright's biographer, John G. Turner, says that Bright wanted to do more than merely evangelize individuals. He sensed that the thousands of students his organization had converted weren't turning the tide or restoring "America to its Christian roots." Bright wanted to offer "evangelical solutions to the nation's ills."[24]

Those ills were on display in Bright's 1986 book *Kingdoms at War: Tactics for Victory in Nine Spiritual War Zones*. (Bright considered sports and science in addition to his original seven.) The first chapter charts a wide-ranging opposition movement meant to defeat Christianity and America: "globalism" in education, "humanistic media programming," and a national "drift" into sexual immorality. The "next five to ten years are critical," Bright asserts, because the "anti-Christian forces have gained so much ground," a warning he had given before. Bright calls for a national change in how we "conduct business, run our government, write our laws," and manage other areas of influence. This change can only occur through victory in a war that has "ever-widening influence on the mind, on the individual, on the family, in the church, and in the various professions." And he challenges readers to choose: You serve either God's kingdom or Satan's kingdom.[25]

A Third Founding Father

Along with Bright and Cunningham, there is often a third person associated with the legend of that August 1975 meeting. In Cunningham's rendition of that meeting, he notes that a month later, his wife Darlene saw on TV (at other times he said she was listening to a radio show) one of the most well-known Christian apologists of the twentieth century, Francis Schaeffer, offer the same list of seven areas of cultural influence. Like Bright and Cunningham, Schaeffer was also known to minister to a youth-oriented crowd. In 1955 he founded L'Abri, a Swiss-based community for seekers, skeptics, and others, usually young, who wanted answers about God. "A drop-by haven for intellectually curious evangelicals," *The New York Times* called it in a 2011 profile of Schaeffer's son, Frank.[26] L'Abri meeting houses would eventually spread globally, and millions would read the elder Schaeffer's books.

Schaeffer's cultural engagement inspired many preachers to engage in politics, including Jerry Falwell, who would go on to found the Moral Majority in 1979. In the '60s, Falwell was set against the mingling of politics and preachers, specifically criticizing Martin Luther King Jr. and his march in Selma. Schaeffer helped Falwell and his fellow conservative Christians see a broader goal beyond simply sharing the gospel. His work emphasized more systemic issues with modern America, including abortion. He called for a return to the Christian foundations he saw at the origins of the United States—and more broadly, Western civilization—by providing a history of how those origins had been abandoned.

Schaeffer was also influential on Cunningham and Bright. In 1968 Schaeffer led a training event for Youth with a Mission in Switzerland where Cunningham started its first school for evangelism. Darlene credits Schaeffer with convincing her and Loren about the importance of the lordship of Christ over all elements of culture. During a trip to Europe in 1971 to celebrate the twentieth anniversary of his organization, Bright arranged a special meeting for his son with Schaeffer. More than a decade later, Bright called Schaeffer "one of the greatest men of our times."[27]

As Bright and Cunningham met in Colorado in August 1975, Schaeffer and his wife were on a European film shoot for his tandem movie-and-book project *How Should We Then Live?*[28] That book included analysis of the kind of topics on the list Cunningham and Bright had given each other. *How Should We Then Live?* is a sweeping intellectual history of the impact of culture—from science to art to music to philosophy to capitalism to politics—on Christianity and its followers since its origin. In a previous book, Schaeffer had outlined the "line of despair"—that point at which a cohesive or unified answer to the accumulation of cultural knowledge is untenable and so the world drifts into secular, even nihilistic hopelessness. That certainly laid the ground for fears of a satanic rule of the world à la Cunningham and Bright.

The book and movie narrated by Schaeffer "became a sensation" in American evangelicalism, historian Daniel K. Williams wrote: "Conservative evangelicals had been looking for an explanation for the secular drift of their country, and Schaeffer's diagnosis of contemporary cultural ills gave them a framework for understanding it." The impact was clear: evangelicals now understood there was a "culture war" taking place in America, "and they were determined to become active participants in it."[29]

Cunningham's criticism of religious enclaves and Bright's call to go beyond individual evangelism mirror Schaeffer's call for a wider interaction with culture. All three rejected fundamentalism's isolationist style and tone. Jimmy Draper, president of the Southern Baptist Convention from 1982 to 1984, said that Schaeffer was "the first one" to clearly lay out the growing danger to Christianity's important role in culture and to say "we need to stand for the things that God has revealed to us."[30] Previewing the stakes laid out by Bright in his 1986 book, in 1981 Schaeffer wrote in *The Christian Manifesto* that "the two world views [Christianity and humanism] really do bring forth with inevitable certainty not only personal differences, but total differences in regard to society, government, and law. There is no way to mix these two total world views. They are separate entities that cannot be synthesized."[31]

While Schaeffer died in 1984, his words remained a powerful driver of evangelical posture toward the larger culture. Before he died, Schaeffer published a scathing critique of evangelical leaders whom he thought hadn't yet taken him to heart. In *The Great Evangelical Disaster*, Schaeffer was particularly critical of Christian leaders who fell into the "blue jean" mindset, a way of accommodating to culture, not confronting it. "I do not think that the evangelical leaders in positions of influence—in schools, in publishing, in other spheres of influence—have been helpful" in confronting the "accepted thought-form of the age around us."[32]

Reconstructing the Spheres

In terms of numbers, Protestants like Bright, Cunningham, and Schaeffer didn't invent the biblical importance of seven. That number in the Hebrew scriptures often is connected to wholeness, completion, perfection, and holiness. The Christian scriptures also use the number seven symbolically, especially in Revelation. In terms of the areas of influence on the original 1975 list, as far back as 1917 theologians noted "five basic institutions of society."[33] In the second half of the twentieth century, sociologists often named family, education, religion, government, and the economy as having a powerful impact on society. Introductory sociology textbooks in the '60s listed those along with science and labor. The *Encyclopedia of Education* in 1971 said these institutions were "discernible in every society, regardless of its degree of complexity."[34]

In 1974 Schaeffer used the label of "spheres" for these social institutions in his keynote presentation at the first global evangelism conference in Lausanne, Switzerland. There Schaeffer framed the gospel as an individual choice but Christianity as a cultural system that claims dominion in all spheres: "If Christianity is truth as the Bible claims, it must touch every aspect of life. If I draw a pie and that pie composes the whole of life, Christianity will touch every slice. At every sphere of our lives Christ will be our Lord and the Bible will be our norm."[35]

Schaeffer was drawing from a broad theology known as Christian reconstructionism, which was forcing the American church to take similar stands on the choices framed by Schaeffer. The movement had as its goal reconstructing for modern use the sets of laws that governed Israel under its kings as laid out in the Jewish scriptures. The group's most well-known publication came two years prior to Bright and Cunningham's meeting with *The Institutes of Biblical Law* by R. J. Rushdoony in 1973. While the book was organized around the Ten Commandments, Rushdoony applied those laws to institutions such as the family, education, the marketplace, and other arenas of our social order.

Rushdoony's impact on Schaeffer, Bright, and Cunningham is clear. A key book by Bright's publishing house—*One Nation under God* by Rus Walton, published in 1975—cited Rushdoony's books and laid out how Christians could apply God's laws to civic life. Schaeffer himself taught one of Rushdoony's early books at L'Abri as early as 1964.[36] As for Cunningham, he began to study reconstructionism in the '80s "with the intent of incorporating" its theology into the training given to his missionaries.[37]

Rushdoony had been writing about the Christian impact on the spheres of cultural life since the early '60s. In 1964 he published a book about the Christian origins of America in which he argued these spheres each had a separate law. This meant that in God's earthly kingdom, "neither church nor state has any right to rule over the spheres, since each is directly under God and equally in the kingdom."[38] This was a direct but uncited reference to a Dutch politician and theologian from the nineteenth century, Abraham Kuyper, from whom Schaeffer also drew. Schaeffer wrote in his 1970 book *Pollution and the Death of Man* that Kuyper taught Christians to see themselves as living in many spheres: "The man in the state, the man who is the employer, the man who is the father, the elder in the church, the professor at the university—each of these is a different sphere. But even though they are in different spheres at different times, Christians are to act like Christians in each of these spheres."[39]

The List Becomes a Mandate

The genealogy of the list is clear. But the ascendancy of the list wasn't always a straight line. The legend of Bright and Cunningham's meeting was born long after it happened. It's always been a curiosity as to why Bright and Cunningham waited more than a decade to write about their lists (and why only the latter ever mentioned in print the 1975 meeting). It could be that by the late '80s when both published their books, others were suggesting similar ideas along with a strong claim to divine approval. One of these was Fuller Seminary professor C. Peter Wagner, a leader in what was then known as the "church growth" movement—a loose collection of pastors and seminary professors who promoted ideas on how to bring new people into the church. As he became popular in the growing field, Wagner turned from a separatist stance against culture to concluding that Christians are God's "chosen agents" to change society. They had a "cultural mandate" to Christianize institutions.[40]

Wagner was not the first to use that phrase. He wrote that he first came across it while reading a 1968 article. It has roots in the Genesis creation story, where God commands the first humans, "Be fruitful and increase in number; fill the earth and subdue it. Rule over the fish in the sea and the birds in the sky and over every living creature that moves on the ground" (Gen. 1:28). Most interpreters focus on humans' power over nature. Kuyper and others defined that call more broadly as a responsibility to maintain cultural goodness, which would impact non-Christians. This is often labeled "common grace."

But Rushdoony and Wagner and their acolytes went even further. Understanding the verse as a Christian social responsibility to serve the poor or feed the hungry wasn't enough. Rushdoony thought his elders in the Reformed movement didn't emphasize enough the power of God's law. And as an emerging charismatic, Wagner said Kuyper erred when he failed to consider the spiritual dimensions of social transformation. Wagner and Rushdoony turned to another translation of the word "rule" in some versions of the Genesis verse: "have dominion."

For Wagner and the charismatics who in the '90s began to form networks with him, having dominion over the world meant identifying demonic institutions and the ideologies—including everything from gang violence to higher education—and making them targets of spiritual warfare, "spiritually mapping" cities to identify areas under satanic influence. Such warfare was conducted through activities like prayer marches through identified areas and calling on demons to leave. The mapping and warfare were empowered by the 1975 list, which Wagner began to mention in his books. He described areas of influence dominated by what he called territorial spirits. These spirits could overcome buildings, seats of government, and neighborhoods, and as sin-filled strongholds they could affect a whole city. Some of the reports Wagner used in his 1995 book about these spirits came from Cunningham's ministry.

Wagner's role in the growth of the seven mountains movement also highlights how the movement has brought together two powerful but often disagreeable Protestant traditions: the Reformed movement led by Schaeffer and Rushdoony and the charismatic movement that included Cunningham and Wagner. Wagner himself said he joined the charismatic camp as he also turned toward the cultural mandate. His new colleagues convinced him the movement needed spiritual leaders who acted like the apostles from the first century of Christianity. Those apostles—named by Wagner as the New Apostolic Reformation—have been instrumental over the years in spreading the mandate movement. To be sure, there were deep divisions in Reformed Christianity over Rushdoony's ideas as well. And Rushdoony also had a falling out with his most prolific follower and son-in-law, Gary North. But whatever their sizable differences in many areas of theology, especially when it came to eschatology (how the world will end), the two groups mingled together in conferences, publications, and desires for dominion in the '80s and '90s. They came to share the list and its mandate.

Heirs Appear

If the plan to Christianize America started with a divine appointment between Loren Cunningham and Bill Bright, the list they created entered the twenty-first century still searching for success—and a consistent metaphor. Then God put Cunningham in another serendipitous meeting. At a conference in British Columbia in 2000 designed to help Christians create wealth, Cunningham ran into a struggling former pastor named Lance Wallnau looking for divine ways to understand the marketplace. Cunningham told Wallnau about his 1975 vision and meeting with Bright. A year later Wallnau met Wagner at another conference and was introduced to Wagner's vast and growing network of apostles and prophets who had begun predicting great societal change.

It is Wallnau who popularized mountains as the dominant metaphor for the movement. Precisely how he came to see that as the needed label is lost in the many versions of the story that Wallnau has told. One version is that a few months prior to speaking with Cunningham, Wallnau heard about a Georgia state senator's deathbed vision of mountains, though Wallnau at times discredits his own telling of that story. And one should not discount the reality that the location in British Columbia where Cunningham and Wallnau met is Kelowna, a city in a valley surrounded by mountains.

Because of the mountain metaphor, Wallnau has long been credited with resurrecting the mandate movement, especially when he took on the leadership of the movement after Wagner died in 2016. Wallnau wrote a book that year about Donald Trump, framing his candidacy as part of a movement to bring a "wrecking ball to political correctness." He followed that up with a similar book in 2020 that claimed to use a biblical "code" to understand contemporary America. He's traveled the globe appearing with a ubiquitous whiteboard covered in the summits of the seven mountains and sells books and videos about the seven mountains on his website. In a 2022 book, Christian nationalism expert Andrew Seidel called Wallnau the "father of American Dominionism."[41] In 2023 Wallnau added an eighth mountain, what he named the "mountain of me," or self-mastery.[42]

Wallnau spent much of 2024 headlining Trump-supportive campaign events with Charlie Kirk. This tour of swing states was not surprising. Wallnau had long supported Kirk as heir to the seven mountains movement. Wallnau said the tour in part happened because he wanted to defend Kirk, who had faced criticism because he was, in Wallnau's words, "the face of Christian Nationalism."[43]

To understand the power of that statement, among others naming Kirk as the heir to the seven mountains movement, one must understand the context of the thoroughly surprising statement Kirk made at that CPAC event in 2020. It was surprising not just because Trump has never mentioned the seven mountains or its mandate in any public manner, but because—up to that point—neither had Kirk.

Kirk has always identified himself as an evangelical Christian. But Turning Point's messages early on were consistently secular, mainly focused on free market values and economic issues, and shying away from any culture war hot buttons like abortion, though he relied early on from donors who wanted to push those buttons.[44] Turning Point and Kirk broke on to the national scene in 2016 with campaigns attacking higher education and the federal government; even then Kirk kept the organization from religion. While Kirk nodded to the Bible in his 2016 debut manifesto, *Time for a Turning Point*, he also claimed that politically aggressive Christian leaders throughout the '70s and '80s tried to wrongly impose their beliefs through government policy. Rather than replicating those errors, Kirk said he advocated for his political positions through a secular worldview because the government established by the founders was also secular. Responding to an interviewer's observation in 2018 that Kirk doesn't proselytize, the young activist said he talked about his faith when asked, but that he saw his job as the face of Turning Point as no different from being a plumber or electrician, who likely doesn't tell everyone they meet about their religion.[45] In 2019 in the premiere episode of his self-named (and now top 10 in downloads) podcast, Kirk denied overlap between his religion and politics: "I'm very careful not to have my religious views and my faith inform my political decisions."[46]

That same year, however, Kirk met a California megachurch pastor named Rob McCoy. McCoy himself was also a convert to the seven mountains movement. Kirk said that over a series of conversations, the pastor began to challenge him to rethink his position separating politics and religion. By April, Kirk and McCoy began sharing stages together, first in California, then nationally in other churches in the Calvary Chapel network, which had been hosting advocates of the seven mountains as far back as 2010. And the mandate movement embraced Kirk just as quickly. Wallnau began promoting Kirk on Twitter, and Kirk had Wallnau on his show. Then came the 2020 CPAC speech in which Kirk linked Trump with the seven mountains movement. Pastors and spiritual advisors around Trump also began claiming Kirk, and by 2021 Kirk began appearing at seven mountains–themed summits and conferences.

Riding the Wave

Turning Point has always had tremendous support from conservative power players. GOP donors Bill Montgomery and Foster Friess were among Kirk's earliest supporters. Ginni Thomas, wife of Supreme Court justice Clarence Thomas, was an early Turning Point advisory board member. But Kirk knew also that the GOP had radically changed when Trump won the nomination in 2016. That summer Kirk befriended Donald Trump Jr. and spent months campaigning with him. That paid off in a massive way. When the elder Trump became president, Turning Point's fundraising skyrocketed. In 2018, according to InfluenceWatch, Turning Point raised over $28 million, compared to $10 million the previous year. According to NBC News, by 2021 Turning Point was reporting $55 million in revenue. Since 2018, Turning Point has hosted Trump fourteen times.

The Biden administration was also great for the group's fundraising. In June 2023, Turning Point reported more than $80 million in revenue, according to tax records. Its political arm, Turning Point Action, began in late 2019 and by 2020 was running a highly sophisticated social media campaign that downplayed the COVID pandemic and sowed doubt about the upcoming election. It ramped up spending in the 2022 election cycle and hosted several conferences and rallies. By 2024 it could be said Turning Point was ruling the party as a whole. Politico noted that long-standing groups such as CPAC had "lost their pull," barely filling their convention ballrooms, while Kirk played a key role in usurping the chairwoman of the GOP, Ronna McDaniel.[47] On the eve of the 2024 election, in which Kirk and Turning Point played essential roles putting Trump back in the White House, the *Atlantic* called Kirk the right's new kingmaker.[48] At a Turning Point fundraiser at Trump's Florida estate in December 2024, Donald Trump Jr. said, "Charlie runs truly one of the finest operations, not just in modern politics, but perhaps ever."

Since embracing the seven mountains movement, Turning Point is no longer merely a youth-oriented group. It has an army of staff in every major city to reach all ages. It has widely expanded its content creation and media capabilities. It hosts women's conferences and men's summits. Turning Point Action has gone on to run multimillion-dollar canvassing campaigns in several election cycles. In 2021 Kirk and McCoy started Turning Point Faith, a branch that targets pastors and their congregations. That has made inroads in charismatic and Baptist churches, two significant parts of the broader American evangelical landscape. And Turning Point Academy has started schools, giving out free curriculum thanks to generous donors.

Kirk has done all this to make Turning Point the indispensable organization for the seven mountains movement. By each of its arms at the same time, Turning Point is fulfilling the mandate. As Kirk said in 2021, "Winning very simply for us is restoring the American way of life."[49] Kirk's plan for restoration is well underway. The picture of victory outlined through each chapter in this book lays bare the danger our nation faces.

Chapter One

God's 1776 Project

The Mountain of Education

In late 2016, a group unknown beyond the fringes of conservative politics wanted to capitalize on the victory of Donald Trump and his plans for America. The group, which had begun a few years prior by attacking higher education, named 200 professors to a "watchlist" to expose their advancement of "leftist propaganda in the classroom."

A year into my job as an English professor in a small Georgia town, at a school I had never heard of before applying, I was added to that list. I was added not because I discriminated against conservative students, but because months earlier I had written an opinion piece for our state's largest newspaper arguing against a law that allows people to carry concealed firearms on college campuses.

This was my first introduction to Turning Point USA, an organization that built itself not only attacking higher education but defending unlimited gun rights. The watchlist caught professors' attention across many other campuses as well. And that was the point. Turning Point's list went viral and drew a lot of media coverage.

When I discovered that the founder of Turning Point was college aged, I thought the list must be like those professor rating sites where often disgruntled students grind their axes. But my colleagues across the nation took the list and Turning Point more seriously. I was wrong and quickly understood why my colleagues invoked McCarthyism. Other professors not named began publicly calling for themselves to be added in solidarity. More than 12,000 professors have signed on to a letter from the national faculty advocacy group asking Turning Point to add their names. Across the years since then, many professors on the list have received hate mail. Today Turning Point's list includes more than 750 names from 400 schools. Graduate teaching assistants to school presidents are named. Some are named for their published academic scholarship, while others are named because of emails they wrote to colleagues or students, often sent to Turning Point through its tip line. One professor is named because she wanted the University of Alabama to remove the word "Dixie" from its fight song. Even as Turning Point says it is targeting liberal indoctrination, the schools on the list range from conservative Christian colleges to the Ivy League, from public to private, and almost every state. There are even a handful of high school teachers on the list.

Turning Point's list echoes a 2006 book by liberal professor turned conservative activist David Horowitz called *The Professors: The 101 Most Dangerous Academics in America*. A colleague in my academic field had been named in that list. Now a decade later I was named to a similar one. Fears of campus indoctrination date much further back, however, to the era when the seven mountains mandate began—long before Turning Point's founder, Charlie Kirk, was even born.

At the time I learned about Kirk, he was barely into his twenties. He had not gone to college due to family financial difficulties. Kirk instead applied to West Point for the taxpayer-subsidized free tuition but was rejected. He declined to enroll at Baylor, the nominally Baptist university in Texas, because he didn't want to take out student loans. The story he tells of the summer after high school suggests that his foray into politics would only last a "gap year."

One might think that not being able to afford college and wanting a degree drives the obvious personal animus Kirk has toward higher education. But it was not jealousy or dreams deferred that drove him. And it was not that admissions decision either. Kirk hates higher education—all public education in fact—because he believes that, as a system, from start to finish, from kindergarten to degree, it indoctrinates students against God and against America. For Kirk, as heir to the seven mountains mandate, educating students about the greatness of America, including its supposed origins and consensus as a Christian nation, is the first step to turning back those schools to God. To turn the schools back to God means to turn the nation back to God. Conquering the mountain of education is doing the Lord's will.

This is why Kirk is so angry at education.

The reason for Kirk's animus is on display each semester as he conducts speaking tours of college campuses, inviting those who disagree with him to the front, only to be "schooled," "burned," or "owned" on video and then used as recurring content on Turning Point's social media platforms. I have sat in the crowd for two of those events, astonished as I watched students cheer when Kirk mocked the education they are getting.

It was on clear display in August 2021 when as a new resident of Scottsdale, Arizona, Kirk stood maskless at a lectern a few feet away from the city's school board. He was there to chastise them over their COVID mask-mandate policy. In shorts fit for the gym, sneakers, and a T-shirt emblazoned with three large red letters that spelled USA on the front, the 6-foot, 4-inch unkempt Kirk angrily told the board members (all masked) that his new town, which leans conservative, felt more like the liberal bastion of San Francisco due to "all of you and your self-righteous measures that you're [taking] to abuse the children of this wonderful state."

Citing statistics as he read from prepared notes on his phone about the impact of the "Chinese coronavirus" on children and claiming the district's mask mandate went against the "will of the taxpayers," Kirk pinched his pointer finger at the members to emphasize his disgust. On its YouTube page, Turning Point described the scene this way: "Charlie goes off." Kirk ended his more than three-minute barrage with a civic threat: "Your time is soon up. The people of this state and this school district are rising up. . . . You have awoken a sleeping giant. I hope you enjoy your masked short-term future while it still lasts."[1]

Kirk's threat is not empty. It is the energy behind Turning Point's sweeping plan to destroy public education, following models and tactics used in the past by other groups pushing their shared desire for more patriotic, religious education. But what separates Turning

Point from other groups is how it has taken on the animus of its founder to such a degree that its efforts to conquer the mountain of education are not aimed at persuasion but punishment. And the punishment is part of the pedagogy. It is supposed to teach like the rod on the child, as the often-quoted proverb says. Unlike previous attacks on education from supporters of the seven mountains mandate, the plan isn't to build a parallel education system where conservative White families can flee the evils of integration and evolution. Turning Point isn't merely interested in expanding Christian schools, recruiting more parents to enroll their children, or for churches to start new schools. Its goal is also to punish public education as a system for curriculum choices that go against God. In a nation whose children and public schools continue to diversify, that might sound like empty rhetoric, anger from a group dedicated to a lost cause. But the seven mountains mandate was never about majority rule. Rather, the vision is for a righteous minority to gain power. In education, this minority will be school board members and principals who are linked to well-funded churches across the nation overseeing a curriculum transformation. This advancing truth will "teach 'em" in more than one way.

The Educational Long Game

For decades, education has been a "long game" for White evangelicals. Many have seen their purpose as being "salt and light" in a dark culture of public schools, perhaps saving a few from within or outlasting its influence using Christian private schools as a bulwark. But there has also been another strategy. In her 2015 book about Christian nationalism, scholar Julie Ingersoll named this strategy as one "designed to build a thoroughly Reconstructed society." This type of society is based on the theology of Christian reconstructionism. The father of that theology, R. J. Rushdoony, laid the foundation for its educational aspect in the '60s through his expert testimony in early lawsuits advocating for what is now known as "school choice." After *Brown v. Board of Education* ordered the desegregation of schools, White conservative Christians created a parallel education system to avoid integration. Even as these people led an exodus from public schools, however, they targeted those same schools, seeking a diversion of public funds into vouchers that could be used for tuition to private schools. As White evangelicals lost their privileged status in public education, some "began to reexamine the foundations of public education," many concluding that "public education is, by definition, unbiblical," Ingersoll notes.[2] In Rushdoony's "reconstructed" society, the government should have no role in education. Instead, it should remain under the auspices of parents and churches. Anything else, he said, would "violate biblical law." This is why Ingersoll wrote that homeschooling is seen as the "single most important tool" for the reconstruction of society.

Rushdoony was influenced by Dutch theologian Abraham Kuyper's cultural spheres of influence, but Rushdoony's plans for education (and those who use the seven mountains metaphor) differ from Kuyper in an important way. Kuyper wrote in his initial lecture on "sphere sovereignty" in 1880 that education should remain sovereign in its own sphere. While Kuyper in that lecture was proposing a Christian or "free" university as an alternative to state or public universities, this equality of spheres meant "neither church, state, or individual rose in authority over the rest of civil society."[3] Kuyper argued for the needed presence of religion in what we might consider public schools, but he was committed to pluralism in all spheres, especially in education. On the other hand, Rushdoony defined education as primarily religious and held that any curriculum not grounded in his religion was not merely secular but anti-Christian. This claim meant that for Rushdoony and his allies, there can be no compromising with advocates of religiously neutral public education.

The Past as Prologue

The theological justification was tied to an eschatological one. The decades-long attack on public education was further fueled by growing end-times pressure. Sociologist Sara Diamond noted this in her groundbreaking analysis of the Christian right, beginning with her 1989 book *Spiritual Warfare*. She wrote about the man who would go on to define end-times rhetoric for the Christian right through best-selling novels and then movies about the future, Tim LaHaye of *Left Behind* fame. In 1970 LaHaye wrote that "humanist domination" was a sign of the end-times, specifically a "seven year period of social chaos preceding Christ's return."[4] This is a reference to a specific eschatology called premillennialism, in which Christians are taken to heaven in a spontaneous action called the "rapture" and society endures a period of "tribulation" marked by widespread violence and societal upheaval. Only after this will Jesus return and reign for a thousand years. This has led many of the followers of that theology to ignore public education and culture writ large on the assumption that believers will soon be whisked away to heaven anyway.

This is why supporters of Christian nationalism argue that among their most important tasks "is overcoming the idea that the world is going to end very soon."[5] Instead, they promote an eschatology in which America will gradually or all at once become ruled over by Christian leaders, setting up a return of Jesus not to that chaos but to a Christian age. In that view, Christians prepare for the return of Jesus by creating a kingdom of God on earth. Ironically, this postmillennial view, in which the world ends *after* Christ's thousand-year reign, was advocated by the progressive reformers of the Social Gospel movement in the late nineteenth and early twentieth centuries and thus opposed by fundamentalists and their evangelical progeny. Some scholars have noted the fierce divide between premillennialist and postmillennialist positions has faded, especially when it comes to countering a growing fear of secularism. In other words, conservatives haven't abandoned their premillennialism; it's just that enemies became more important.

After Rushdoony, for much of the '80s the attack on education centered on "secular humanism." It was something Christians in this era thought was permeating public education. In his 1986 book *Kingdoms at War: Tactics for Victory in Nine Spiritual War Zones*, Campus Crusade founder Bill Bright argued that this takeover began as early as the nineteenth century. Bright summarized a litany of reports and studies—mainly the dramatic 1983 "A Nation at Risk" report from the Department of Education—contrasting the current supposed crisis with what Bright claimed was the original purpose of education in the American colonies: "communicating Calvinist Puritan religion from one generation to the next." That sense of inheritance as part of American education was corrupted in the 1830s, Bright said, when educational reformer and noted "father" of the common school movement Horace Mann began organizing "a centralized, state-controlled school system" in Massachusetts. According to Bright, Mann was influenced by a British "social reformer" who aimed to replace religion with what Bright labeled a "humanistic philosophy" that had subsequently taken over public education. Aiming his words at contemporary times, Bright assailed teacher unions and declared that parents, not the state, were responsible for their children's education. Bright encouraged parents not only to be active in their child's classrooms but to campaign for their local school boards to "actively work to influence their educational system."[6]

More than twenty years later, the Pentecostal pastor and prophet Johnny Enlow, who embraced the seven mountains mandate by name in several of his books, repeated nearly theme for theme Bright's words in a 2008 book called *The Seven Mountain Prophecy*. He claimed that Western education had been "infiltrated and taken over by forces opposed to those originally intended to be there." He too recounted the early years of education in America, noting they were meant to "serve as places of training and admonition in the fear of God." In a common occurrence among those in the second generation of the seven mountains movement, Enlow went further than Bright in naming that which was corrupting education. While both men cited "humanism," Enlow claimed that it and other "isms" in the culture in his era were being pushed by "demonic principalities and powers" or "spiritual wickedness in high places." He names those powers directly as either an ally of Satan or Satan himself, who "sits at the top of the mountain." While Bright encouraged civic action, Enlow called for wholesale reform and erasure of this "demonic" system. He wanted teachers who would represent the kingdom of God but said that "having spiritually gifted teachers throughout the system isn't enough; the certification system and the curriculum itself must be overhauled."[7]

From the Start

If Enlow is the second generation, then Kirk is an heir from the third. His angry tirade in Scottsdale makes clear that like others before him, he is trying to turn White evangelical eschatological indifference into an aggressive attempt at restoration of what he has called an "America-loving education system." What is different for Kirk's generation is that the parallel education system once seen as a bulwark against cultural change is now an offensive weapon to end the culture war, to conquer this particular mountain.

This kind of attitude toward public schools was always in the DNA of Turning Point because it was the key theme in the Kirk origin story. In April 2012, during his senior year in a suburban Chicago public high school, Kirk wrote an article for the alt-right site Breitbart in which he accused his teachers of liberal indoctrination. While it's hard to know how many people saw the article, any article published by Breitbart is going to ricochet across the conservative internet. Kirk wrote another in June about Obama and the "youth vote." By July he was on Fox News. Kirk founded Turning Point that summer.

In that first Breitbart piece, Kirk specifically attacked a textbook used in Advanced Placement economics. Kirk claimed that because the book didn't give enough space to his favorite conservative economic theories, it was "propaganda" and that the use of it "will create a youth so misinformed and clueless that they will have no choice but to turn to the government. And that is exactly what the liberals want." Kirk had been known to debate his teachers about politics. He told the *Chicago Tribune* in 2018 that sometimes teachers would kick him out of class for arguing.[8] Kirk has been arguing with schools ever since. His 2021 speech to the school board is emblematic of the tactics by his organization. In May 2022 he and Turning Point supported a group of Scottsdale moms who had sued a school district for "targeting and harassing" conservative parents. Kirk called for "the eradication of the Deep State's unprecedented targeting of everyday moms, dads, and students who dare to love America."[9] If local school boards, administrators, librarians, and of course teachers won't educate God's way, then Kirk and Turning Point will bring

God's judgment upon them. That judgment aims to purify education and return the nation's public schools to their colonial roots and so to build God's kingdom through God's pedagogy.

A Model for the Plan

Turning Point learned that pedagogy from a small private college in Michigan. For decades, Hillsdale College stood as the quintessential example of the parallel Christian education institution. It has long refused federal student loans because of the strings attached. But in the last decade or so, Hillsdale has created a network of private schools using its K–12 curriculum and has aimed to partner with public charter schools and districts. Hillsdale's map of member schools lists more than twenty schools in fourteen states as of March 2024. In 2023, Republican South Dakota governor Kristi Noem consulted with Hillsdale faculty when setting new state standards for social studies curriculum. In Florida, Republican governor Ron DeSantis referenced Hillsdale as he boasted of overhauling the state's education system.[10] Likewise, Tennessee's GOP governor has "courted" Hillsdale and its curriculum that emphasizes "America's strengths rather than its shortcomings."[11]

To spread their doctrine to the general public, Hillsdale offers free online courses to all who want them. These courses mirror the curriculum sent to school districts, though they end with no actual college credit. There are literature courses on Jane Austen, Mark Twain, and "the great books" of the Western tradition. Courses on modern politics include one on the "decline" of American citizenship that claims to teach how "the disappearance of sovereign borders" and "the growth of the deep state" help to form a "global government." The course "The American Left: From Liberalism to Despotism" claims to teach the "philosophical origins of America's radical movements and how they have overtaken America's institutions." The trailer video for a course on civil rights in American history references the 2020 protests in response to the murder of George Floyd through images of burning cars and American flags. A narrator speaking over those images says in the beginning of the video that the claim America is "infected with systemic anti-black racism is a lie." Contrasting those images with video of Martin Luther King Jr. and the civil rights era, the video argues that "identity politics" is a danger to freedom and the rights gained during that time. The video says that the educational system in America should "do justice" to the nation's past and teach it to emphasize our common humanity, not racial differences.[12]

Kirk learned the Hillsdale model directly from Hillsdale's president, Larry Arnn, as the two served together on the short-lived 1776 Commission, which began in the last months of the first Trump administration. (The commission had its only meeting on January 5, 2021, and released its report on January 18, Martin Luther King Jr. Day. Kirk's name does not appear on the final report, which suggests he resigned from the commission at some point.) The commission was a direct reply to the 1619 Project, a *New York Times Magazine* project led by journalist Nikole Hannah-Jones, which sought to center slavery in the origins of America. Hannah-Jones and the *Times* won a Pulitzer Prize in 2020 for the project, the name of which refers to the year the first enslaved Africans arrived in Virginia.

By contrast, the 1776 Commission aimed to make public schools more patriotic and religious, what it called a "restoration of American education." The commission's report claimed that the nation's founding fathers' "ingenious division of church and state was neither to weaken the importance of faith nor to set up a secular state, but to open up the public space of society to a common American morality." This "common morality" is to be paired with a "sense of enlightened patriotism" that has been erased by a "legacy of anti-Americanism" in education that includes progressivism, communism, and fascism, inherently and implicitly atheistic enterprises.[13]

Arnn has long been a central figure in conservative politics and its policy on education. Before coming to Hillsdale in 2000, he was one of four founders of and eventually ran the Claremont Institute in California, a conservative think tank that gave some intellectual vision to the conservative political resurgence in the '80s and '90s. In this century, especially since Trump came into politics, the institute has given itself over to the culture war, spreading the notion of a dual importance of divine law and natural law in our constitutional balance. One of its leaders was John Eastman, who famously wrote in the waning days of the Trump administration memos arguing that the vice president could ignore the Electoral College. He was later charged by prosecutors in Fulton County, Georgia, in a 2020 election conspiracy case. The Claremont Institute named Kirk one of its fellows in 2021.

As Arnn is a product of Claremont's philosophy, Kirk is a product of Arnn. In a 2021 *Human Events* piece, Kirk mentions he had been viewing Arnn's lectures about Aristotle, part of the online course about Aristotle's *Nicomachean Ethics*.[14] In that piece and other places, Kirk uses Aristotle to wed religion and politics, specifically seeing the church as a governmental authority.

Selling the Plan

To implement his vision for education, in June 2022 Kirk hired long-time Christian school administrator Hutz Hertzberg as head of Turning Point's educational arm, Turning Point Academy. It sought to reclaim education by reviving virtuous education and restoring God as the foundation of education. Silver haired, tall, and thin, the polished sixty-five-year-old veteran of Christian education at all levels sounds and dresses akin to Arnn. And he has a similar resume. Hertzberg worked as the executive pastor of the Moody Church in Chicago alongside its well-known lead pastor Erwin Lutzer, who is a noted author in evangelical publishing circles. Before that, Hertzberg worked in higher education administrative and faculty positions at leading evangelical institutions.

What drew Kirk's attention was Hertzberg's most recent role as president of Christian Heritage Academy, a preK–12 college preparatory school in Northfield, Illinois. The school was started by another well-known evangelical author, Wayne Grudem, in 1984. And more than a decade later, Kirk was one of its students. It's where Kirk said he became a Christian in fifth grade.[15]

Like Kirk, Hertzberg pushes the idea that the public school environment stands against Christians. He told a story to a Christian radio show in October 2023 about a student named "Tom" who went to Christian Heritage through eighth grade but then on to a public high school. Hertzberg asked Tom's mother some weeks into the school year how Tom was doing. The mother responded that her son had learned "that if he's going to get through he can't talk about his faith." Hertzberg said that was "tragic" because there was a time in the past when he as a young student could "bring [his] faith to bear in a public school. But that day is long gone." Hertzberg called the present moment in public education a "911 moment" because the neutrality of public schools is over. Christian students are "shut down. They're marginalized. They're ostracized. There is no opportunity really in most cases to bring your light to bear in the public school setting."[16]

The claim about a loss of neutrality—where the public school system actively promotes a religion and demands Christians be silent—has been a talking point for evangelicals for decades. Grudem wrote a school brochure in 1982 that noted that "if we keep our children in public schools, they will be trained year after year to keep their Christianity just where our society says it 'belongs'—at home and in church—in *private*, where it will not be noticed, and where it will have little effect on our politics, our laws, our corporations, our universities, our news media, or our nation's public conscience." In other words, "secular education trains children to be secularized Christians."[17] Speaking to an audience of pastors in 2023, Hertzberg said there was much "demonic" activity in public schools. He recommended to the audience that they try to better understand the "intentional indoctrination of the sexualization of our students." Hertzberg said this indoctrination dates to Alfred Kinsey, the famous professor at Indiana who studied sex in the '40s and '50s.[18]

There is an obvious difference between Kirk's own high school history—which had nothing to do with religion, in Kirk's telling of it—and Hertzberg's story about "Tom." But their audiences see them as part of the same narrative about loss. This sense of loss certainly has pushed many to private schools. But the sense of loss is also a call to convince a new generation of evangelicals long accustomed to abandoning public schools to retake them for good, for the good of the nation.

Weaponizing Scripture to Pronounce Judgment

Kirk knows that call best resonates when it comes from pastors. To get a sense of how Turning Point convinced pastors to partner with it to save education, one can listen to how these pastors justify such a partnership to their congregation. These pastors often employ warrants that suggest the church needs to save more than just the children in their church. But unlike previous decades of such rhetoric, the impact of such a salvation has been scaled up as systemic issues in need of addressing for the sake of the community become more threatening. The implication is, of course, to rebuild the system with God's blueprints.

In August 2023, Vintage Church in Harker Heights, Texas, became a "proud" partner of Turning Point when it began its academy.[19] Vintage's pastor, Stephen Martin, said in a video about starting the church's school that he had mistakenly "outsourced the education of [his] children to the government." What he thought were "good schools" in Texas were actually revealed to him during the pandemic era to be the opposite. But most importantly, individual Christian parents trying to be a barrier against the hours spent in these schools were ineffective. "Trying to reform this system with our kids in it is like taking a Nerf gun to fight with the Death Star," he said. He framed that parental battle as "the 16,000-hour war," referring to what he said are the number of school hours from kindergarten to twelfth grade during which kids are exposed to "the secular progressive strategy to indoctrinate our children."[20] It is not enough for Christian parents to "simply take our children out of public education," Martin said. They must "understand how this war is being waged" so they can "protect" children, presumably not just their own.[21]

In a sermon on the state of education, part of a sermon series titled "Under God," Martin heavily implied that public schools were a systemic threat to the nation as a Christian order because of "a secular worldview" being taught to young people. The pastor claimed there had been a "long march through the institutions" of society, especially educational ones, by "Marxist-inspired" education "experts with pink hair" who are introducing "crazy ideas" not "ordained by

God." While inviting people to enroll their children in his church's school, he also claimed that Protestants like him had abandoned public schools: "We've just kind of let the government step in under some guise of separation of church and state."[22]

The sermon was centered on the book of Daniel, making an explicit analogy between the United States and Babylon, the land Daniel and other Jews were exiled to. The pastor likens the American educational system to the Babylonian system Daniel was educated in. This analogy has several flaws. First, while the pastor claims the "teenager" Daniel was chosen by Babylonian leaders because children "don't know anything," the text indicates that Daniel was chosen because he showed "aptitude for every kind of learning" and was "well informed, quick to understand" (Daniel 1:4). Second, while the Babylonians educated Daniel in their language and literature, which the pastor implies was indoctrination, the text indicates Daniel did not renounce his faith and in fact refused to "defile" himself with royal food and wine. If the intent was indoctrination, it failed.

The pastor ends on a call to action. Not surprisingly he urges parents to remove their children from public schools. But he reveals the plan for education by the seven mountains mandate: "We're not responsible for the country. But we are responsible for our communities, our families, our churches." While this pastor limits the scope of the impact of the new school to the community and not the country, there are many more pastors partnering with Turning Point saying the same thing. And those add up nationally.

This urgency for manifesting judgment can be seen in the rhetoric used as justification by Turning Point. At the bottom of the home page of Turning Point Academy is a quote: "Silence in the face of evil is itself evil: God will not hold us guiltless. Not to speak is to speak. Not to act is to act." Turning Point credits the words to Dietrich Bonhoeffer, the German pastor made famous for resisting Hitler before and during World War II. He was hanged near the end of the war. Yet Bonhoeffer never said those words. And in fact, Bonhoeffer scholars say it doesn't even sound like him.[23] Using Germany during Hitler's era to illustrate America today is a common move by Turning Point. The organization and Kirk himself have promoted conservative pundit Eric Metaxas's writings about Bonhoeffer. Yet

Bonhoeffer's family and scholars have said Metaxas is twisting Bonhoeffer's writings.[24]

Watchlists

Turning Point has a multipronged attack plan for public education. Six months after Kirk visited the Scottsdale school board as noted in the beginning of this chapter, Turning Point started what it calls a school board "watchlist," modeled after its professor watchlist. This new list called out boards that oversee schools that teach "radical and false ideologies" and hopes to push parents to end the "radical indoctrination of our children in the classroom."[25] The list names districts, board members, and schools. For example, there are more than 240 school districts in Arizona, and the Turning Point list includes more than 40, or one-sixth, of them. Some districts are described as receiving complaints from parents about issues from curriculum to public meeting access. But for other districts, Turning Point lists no reason to call them "radical," only listing the photo and contact information of board members. In some cases, Turning Point has merely copied and pasted the board member's biography from the district's page, citing it as a source. In the case of Bobby Bauders, for example, who sits on the Apache Junction Unified School District in Arizona, the biography lists no policy difference or even negative description to merit inclusion on a "radical" list.

These efforts seek to harass and expel educators, especially those who are trying to expand curriculum, and discourage people willing to be teachers. And they have been effective amid a growing teacher shortage. According to surveys of teachers in 2022, 73 percent of teachers and 85 percent of principals reported that they had experienced "acute job-related stress" during the past semester (compared to an average of just over 35 percent of all working adults).[26]

Vouchers

As heir of the seven mountains mandate, Kirk has turned the White evangelical "long game" into a quicker, direct assault on public education. That strategy has been timed perfectly to align itself with a recent push in state legislatures for what are known as school vouchers—paying individual student tuition at private schools through public tax dollars. The concept of vouchers has been popular in conservative policy since the Reagan administration. But conservative lawmakers have fought to expand those programs in recent years. As of 2023 there were twenty-five voucher programs in sixteen states, mainly Southern and led by GOP legislatures.[27] Those programs give billions in subsidies to nearly a million students. Kirk has long supported vouchers.[28] The school Turning Point named as its first partner, Dream City Christian School in Arizona, has used more than $2 million in state vouchers since Arizona's expanded program took effect in 2022, according to state data. That has, according to an analysis by CNN, likely sapped millions of dollars from the nearby public district's budget.[29] As of the summer of 2024, of the forty-one Christian schools in Turning Point Academy's network, twenty-six are in states with private school voucher programs.[30]

It should come as no surprise that studies of such programs show the large majority of benefactors are not students leaving public schools but students who have never been.[31] In other words, supporters of school vouchers are not merely using the policy to "save" some students from godless public schools, but to defund the entire endeavor. Arizona is a prime example of the monetary effects of these programs. In 2024 the state faced a $1.3 billion budget shortfall, and much of that was due to vouchers. Arizona's program is the "most expansive private school voucher program in the country and is expected to cost more than $900 million" in 2024, "15 times more than initially projected." Cuts to higher education and other public programs are likely.[32]

It's not only a defunding operation. It also is being used to spread the ideology associated with the seven mountains mandate. In a July 2023 report, the Network for Public Education, a pro–public school research group, identified a growing number of charter schools imbued with Christian nationalist ideologies and being used as "weapons of the Right" in their efforts to undermine public schools and reverse social progress. The report identified 273 currently open charter schools featuring curriculum and/or websites "designed to attract white conservative families." An astounding 47 percent of those schools were founded in the time since Donald Trump took office in 2017.[33]

Curriculum

Many charter schools feature a "classical education" model, an approach that dates to medieval times and has roots in ancient Greece and the beginning of rhetoric as a civic skill. One of the "classical schools" that began this trend is the Logos School in Moscow, Idaho, started in the 1980s by Christ Church, which is led by Douglas Wilson, a noted advocate of Christian nationalism. Hillsdale Classical Schools defines a classical education as one that leads students "toward moral and intellectual virtue by means of a rich and robust course of study in the liberal arts and sciences, with instruction in the principles of moral character and civic virtue."[34]

But "classical" is now not limited to private schools. The Oklahoma Department of Education announced in July 2024 that it would revise its social studies curriculum to align with the "classical" model. It enlisted several well-known conservatives, including media influencer Dennis Prager and "historian" David Barton to lead the revision. Prager is the man behind PragerU, which is not a university but a collection of short videos that teach conservative ideology about American history and economics, among other topics. Several states run by conservatives have approved these videos for use in their schools. Not surprisingly, Turning Point sponsored a breakout session at the 2024 Administrators Conference organized by the Oklahoma Department of Education. The superintendent of Oklahoma's public schools, Ryan Walters, is a staunch defender of vouchers and appeared at a Turning Point campus event at Oklahoma State in 2024.

Turning Point calls its schools "5Cs" schools, which stands for "classical, Christian, conservative, church-based, and cost-affordable." Turning Point Academy pushes curriculum designed "to glorify God and preserve the founding principles of the United States."[35] Only in its infancy, as of August 2024, the Turning Point Academy Association map lists forty-one schools that have agreed with its statement of values and that as part of the association have access to Turning

Point curriculum and training.[36] Turning Point suggests it has more than 140 "affiliated" schools nationwide. California has the most with forty-two.

Turning Point's curriculum includes "The Patriots' Catechism," a set of questions and answers about the Constitution designed for easy memorization and quick exposure to the history of American greatness. The curriculum also includes a high school course on "biblical economics" and a course that will help students understand current events "in light of history and through the truth of Scripture."[37] Its "study hall" web page recommends books authored by a Fox News anchor and conservative think tanks. Turning Point also tells schools that they can use its materials in any part of their curriculum.

As of August 2024, four such schools on Turning Point's map were listed as models, labeled with red stars. These models offer evidence for what kind of students and political agenda Turning Point wants to promote. The website of that first partner, Dream City Christian School, says that the school builds "strong, Christian leaders" who will "reject non-Biblical, immoral ideology," which is implicitly the cause of America's current "political and spiritual turmoil." The school, linked with the Assemblies of God megachurch by the same name, proudly displays its link with Turning Point on its website. Turning Point's "flagship" 5C school, Classical Consortium Academy in Barrington, Illinois, also is a "proud" Turning Point model. Its founder and head of school is also director of academics for Turning Point Academy. Begun in 2006, Classical Consortium Academy is a hybrid school that meets in person one or two days a week and the rest at home. While this setup can be cost-effective for the school and therefore more affordable for a family, the move from public charter schools to private schools to hybrid home schools lessens state and federal oversight even more.

Classical Consortium Academy frames its curriculum around grammar, logic, and rhetoric, known as the medieval trivium. Students up to second grade memorize key Bible verses and learn phonics and Latin. In sixth grade students learn grammar, science, and history from well-known home-school curriculum brands. In seventh and eighth grades they learn Christian history, formal logic, and a rhetorical education known as the *progymnasmata*. High school offers courses on a Christian worldview, economics, and apologetics (defending the Christian faith). In economics, students read a primer on the subject written by an economist linked to the conservative Austrian school of economics. In biology, students use a textbook that teaches "scientific principles while seeing evidence of God's creation."[38] In chemistry, students learn how "the details of atomic structure to the makeup of the very air that we breathe . . . [show] us the marvelous handiwork of God."[39]

These are all typical lessons in home-school and Christian school curriculums and have been for decades. But there is a significant difference between the church and Turning Point. Classical Consortium Academy operates out of the Village Church of Barrington, which is part of the Evangelical Free Church of America, a denomination known for its conservative theology. But unlike Turning Point, the EFCA denies tenets of Christian nationalism. While the EFCA affirms that "advocating for God-honoring public policies is one way for us, as Christians, to seek the common good and welfare of all people," it rebukes as "wrong and idolatrous" any notion that "the federal government should declare the United States a Christian nation" or that Americans are "God's chosen people."[40]

The school's choices for textbooks from the American literature canon also show how it isn't a perfect model for Turning Point. Its 2024–2025 book list includes traditional readings for high school students such as *The Scarlet Letter* and *Narrative of the Life of Frederick Douglass*. It is not without irony that these two books are often removed from school library shelves after (usually conservative) parental complaints. And it is even more ironic that as the rise of book bans in public schools has reached a fever pitch in recent years, Turning Point has promoted the efforts of a Black pastor from North Carolina who travels the nation reading explicit language from books at school board meetings and then getting arrested when he refuses to stop.[41]

Higher Values

While Turning Point has targeted K–12 schools through school boards and the academy program, it also continues to attack higher education in ways beyond the "watchlist" noted in the introduction to this chapter. Kirk has said many times that what happens on campus doesn't stay on campus. In other words, the curriculum, lectures, and opinions echo throughout the nation. This is why, when Turning Point targets an individual professor for their views, the organization also challenges the school for allowing such views. This may sound like a strange tactic from an organization that advocates for free speech on campus. But the hypocrisy notwithstanding, the strategy resembles the organization's strategy for K–12 schools: framing curriculum and employment in public education based on values—values as defined by a specific version of Christianity. And professors stand against those values.

Kirk and Turning Point also have taken direct action against college budgets. Over the years Kirk has lambasted the student loan industry and advocated directly to college students that some degrees are worthless, general education courses are pointless, and one doesn't need a degree to be successful in life, himself being a prime example. At one point, Turning Point campaigned to defund universities by convincing alumni not to give.

Turning Point also has taken direct action against professors. In April 2024 two Turning Point employees admitted guilt to defer prosecution for misdemeanor assault and harassment after their arrest for an encounter with an Arizona State University professor in October 2023. The employees—one a camera operator and the other the host of a Turning Point "investigation" show called *Frontlines*—followed the professor around campus, badgering him with questions.[42] At one point the *Frontlines* host accused the professor of wanting to "see a different America exist," presumably because of the professor's advocacy for pro-LGBTQ policies and work to establish the Arizona chapter of Drag Queen Story Hour.[43] According to Inside Higher Ed, a news site that covers colleges, "the confrontation eventually turned physical, ending with" the professor "posting a photo of himself with blood on one side of his face."[44]

These tactics are not new. There is a reason that Vintage Church pastor Stephen Martin chose Daniel in the lion's den as his metaphor for public education. Since fundamentalism emerged more than a century ago, it has been the metaphor for Christians spreading myths about atheist faculty deconverting Christian students or of Christian teens "losing their faith." And this has grown into the broader myth of liberal professors as they have become an effective foil for supporters of Christian nationalism and the seven mountains mandate. In his 2008 book, mandate advocate Johnny Enlow bemoaned the faded origins of several Ivy League schools in training ministers and claimed, "We are, in essence, releasing our young people into humanistic (often atheistic) indoctrination by letting them attend the country's oldest and most respected universities."[45]

Bill Bright once said if he had to start Campus Crusade over again, he would try to do more to evangelize professors. He explained that "the reason for many of the problems in elementary and secondary education" came from the fact that teachers were trained in colleges "permeated with humanistic philosophy." That is why Bright wanted Campus Crusade to start its own graduate school for training Christians entering professions like teaching, medicine, and law—to "help restore them to the moral foundation on which they started."[46] That dream never materialized, but Bright's organization eventually had many programs, conferences, and websites dedicated to evangelizing college faculty. Contrary to Turning Point's war on professors (and Bright's own lament that he should have done more), one of Bright's biographers notes that his ministry "challenges the dominant narrative of the secularization of higher education," and his career demonstrated "how Campus Crusade helped reestablish evangelical Christianity as a visible subculture on American campuses."[47]

Unlike other advocates of the seven mountains mandate, Turning Point has not started a university. But Kirk helped begin a culture war center at a school started for the purpose of retaking the mountain of education. In 1971 the Reverend Jerry Falwell began what was then called Liberty Baptist College through funds generated from his national broadcast *The Old-Time Gospel Hour*. Falwell wanted Liberty to be a beacon for fundamentalist Christians where they could train to be conservative leaders in areas of influence, battling threats to American Christianity. Starting Liberty showed how Falwell was trying to redefine what was then called fundamentalist Christianity, especially in education. In a time when many fundamentalists were retreating from culture and American politics, Falwell was a well-known "public-facing" fundamentalist who thought "although the world would soon face the Rapture and the wrath of God, Christians should still try to influence their society and so perhaps avoid the worst of what was to come."[48] Under the guidance of his son, Jerry Falwell Jr., Liberty has become not merely a nationally known Christian university but a partner with Kirk. Liberty gave Kirk an honorary degree in 2019, and he was one of two namesakes used for its think tank called the Falkirk Center, started that same year. It was renamed the Standing for Freedom Center after the other namesake, Falwell Jr., left in the wake of a sex scandal.

An Educated Public

American democracy isn't merely the value of voting or electing our leaders. Democracy is the informed debate about policies and values, good-faith discourse about our disputed history and disputed moral codes, especially in a religiously pluralistic society. This is why education matters in a democracy.

It is telling that beyond its empty support of free speech, Turning Point hasn't centered democracy in its attack on education. It hasn't made promoting democracy a goal. In fact, Kirk has promoted the idea that America is a republic, not a democracy, a claim promoted by Christian nationalism and its distorted history of our past. Kirk and Turning Point don't want debate. They want divine inspiration to settle all debate. That finally will teach 'em.

Chapter Two

Counselor to the King

The Mountain of Government

In January 2024, Georgia congresswoman Marjorie Taylor Greene—a supporter of Christian nationalism with allies in the seven mountains mandate movement—posted on the social media site formerly known as Twitter that America needed a "national divorce," splitting along red state (i.e., conservative, Republican-dominant) and blue state (progressive, Democrat-dominant) lines. She was responding to a Fox News tweet about the growing number of conservative states supporting Texas in its moves against the federal government over border policy.

It was not the first time the provocative conservative had mentioned this divisive metaphor. In fact, it was the fourth time in about two years she had posted about the possibility.[1] In December 2021, she noted conservatives fleeing blue states and the following October posted about vaccine mandates in some of those states. And in February 2023, she shared on Twitter a seemingly unprompted gripe about Democratic policies being "shoved down our throats": "We need to separate by red states and blue states and shrink the federal government."

While the division talk is new, the downsizing opinion is not. Since the '70s, White evangelicals as politically conservative actors have argued for a massive reduction in the size of the federal government.

From eliminating departments to erasing entitlement programs to slashing spending, they have argued that our Constitution calls for more state power. And of course, in American history, "states' rights" has been a pretext for oppression of racial minorities. Many of those same White evangelicals who support the rights of states also support the seven mountains mandate. This is not a coincidence. The political goal has a theological mandate. They want to undermine the role of the federal government to smooth the way for the installation of biblical governments across America. These governments are not merely grounded in Christian values. They are to be governed by Christians, and Greene's national divorce gives them the best chance to see their goals achieved.

Biblical Government and Voting Rights

After the 2023 social media moment, some accurately labeled Greene's comments a call for civil war. The next day she was a guest on Charlie Kirk's radio show to put out the fire she started.[2] Instead, she poured gasoline on it and suggested that the way forward for the nation was to destroy democracy. To understand Greene's suggestion, one has to understand Kirk's question that prompted it.

Kirk described his fear that people from the blue states wouldn't stop trying to invade the red states, moving and bringing with them progressive policy opinions. The tyrannical governments of blue states (or the federal government) will not stop at state lines. The devil must have dominion. Kirk wanted to know from Greene what conservatives should do about that. In Kirk's mind, red states are threatened by an offensive attack, an invasion by a demonic force. The cultural or political aggression Kirk perceives from Democrats is grounded in language of spiritual warfare, the kind of warfare against government that has defined the mountain of government since the mandate movement began.

To Kirk, then, playing defense isn't enough.

Greene's response to Kirk was as theocratic as it gets. She suggested that those blue people can move to red states, but the red states should regulate their voting. Those people should be banned from voting in state elections for five years. This "cooling-off period," as Kirk described it, might then convince these Democrats to come to their senses and switch parties, or at least stop them from remaking red states into blue ones.

Kirk called Greene's idea a good "thought experiment," which may sound like Kirk is dismissive, but he said similar things in 2021. At a speech on the campus of Missouri State, Kirk said it was immoral for Democrats who move to red states to try to change their new state because their state actually represents the "basic American value system."[3] Kirk didn't do much that day in Missouri to define that value system, merely naming it a form of "patriotism." But his response to Greene two years later showed that a debate about federalism (which is what Kirk labeled the whole segment) was actually a red herring for enforcing "biblical" policies at all costs, even at the cost of constitutional rights.

As one can see from this interaction between Kirk and Greene, Turning Point's plan for the mountain of government doesn't aim merely to win the next election. It is far more sweeping, because it must be far more sustainable than one election. There is only one option for the mountain of government: destroy democracy for God.

One way to get that done has been a strategy by the mandate movement since its beginning: elect its acolytes to leadership positions and have them influence the institution. Greene is one example of this. But the best example is the elevation of Rep. Mike Johnson from Louisiana to Speaker of the House in 2023. In his first week on the job, he displayed the "Appeal to Heaven" flag, which has great symbolic meaning for the movement, outside his new office.[4] Beyond the individual success, the seven mountains mandate defines its conquering the mountain of government in broader cultural change. Having those individuals in power merely cut off funding won't deter the tyrannical, demonic nature of government. This requires a kind of spiritual warfare that sees democracy as a threat. For all its talk about the threat of big government and its creeping bureaucracy, the seven mountains mandate's plan for government is to put it everywhere, involve it in every area of culture. That is because it's God's government the movement wants.

The First Generation

Each of the three men associated with the 1975 Colorado list of seven areas of cultural influence—which became the seven mountains—certainly wanted limited civil government. But they also wanted to return biblical government to its rightful place in our nation, casting aside forms of tyranny brought on by secularism. For example, Loren Cunningham wrote in *Winning God's Way* that his vision was "Bible-based forms of government." Bill Bright likewise wrote that the government should establish a legal system "based on biblical principles." He argued that if Christians "assume the mandate given by Christ to take dominion" specifically over civil government, they could reclaim the world for God.[5] And while he wasn't in Colorado in 1975, Francis Schaeffer also argued that America could and should return to its Christian roots and operate its government from a Christian consensus.

R. J. Rushdoony, leader of the Christian reconstructionism movement most known for its mandate for the Bible to rule America, thought democracy had a key flaw. He dismissed democracy because it replaced God with humans as the central authority. This is why Rushdoony advocated for "sphere law." He wrote, "Every area has its own law-sphere, and every area its own powers as well as God-imposed restraints on its powers. The unity of these activities and spheres is not in any one of them, in man, or in the whole, but is transcendental; it is in God only." And so it is only "totalitarianism, civil or ecclesiastical," that "claims institutional divinity and authority."[6]

One of Rushdoony's most well-known students, Gary North, wrote in a 1986 "biblical blueprint" for a Christian America that such a reconstruction would not impose "some sort of top-down bureaucratic tyranny in the name of Christ." Such would only come through a "bottom-up society" that rests on "self-government under God." But this, as North admits, relies on "majority rule" by Christians.[7] North was willing to admit that the majority may not occur. The bottom from which the society would rise from seemingly was a minority of Christians who read North and Rushdoony. How that minority rule happens in a democracy comes in part through the influence of individuals like Greene and Johnson winning key positions in leadership. Those people in power then claim a power stronger than government to overrule the majority. This undermines democracy and its consent of the governed. Seth Cotlar, a professor of history at Willamette University, notes that supporters of the broader ideology of Christian nationalism often paint secular democracy as the enemy of Christianity, then claim "the only patriotic way to save America from godless secularists was to vote for leaders who would ignore the rules of democracy."[8]

Mapping the Spheres

While Rushdoony gave the seven mountains movement a focus on institutions, with specific emphasis on government, the movement also repurposed the traditional practice of Christian evangelism to spread the mandate and its minority rule. At a global evangelism conference in Lausanne in 1974 led by Billy Graham and Francis Schaeffer, participants debated the value of social reform as part of the gospel message. Some criticized Graham for wasting resources on his stadium crusades—which had the potential to create a majority—and tied evangelism to a kind of cultural understanding that would empower a minority of Christians to take over cities.

Merely reaching your neighbor turned into reaching "people groups," and with that came the need to "unlock the cultural puzzle of the group to which an individual belongs."[9]

One of the attendees of that 1974 meeting was Fuller Theological Seminary church growth professor C. Peter Wagner. By the movement's second conference fifteen years later in the Philippines, Wagner had begun to emphasize the cultural mandate to engage and dominate every area of culture. The move from understanding cultural puzzles to seeing those pieces as obstacles to the gospel meant for Wagner a turn to spiritual warfare against those obstacles. Spiritual warfare was based in desperate pleading with God for change but grew to include declaring impotent anti-Christian forces working against the gospel. For example, the group Intercessors for America in 1986 "systematically targeted" cities across America and documented "negative elements" such as "slavery, racial conflicts," and other "corrupt practices" that had become "strongholds" in the cities and inflicted spiritual "wounds" upon them.[10]

In the '90s, this spiritual warfare effort turned its focus to large metropolitan areas in the United States and the demonic powers that ruled cities. These demons were named through a process called spiritual mapping that "changed the methods of conversion by increasing the scale of conversion and replacing the individual experience with the collective."[11] The person who coined the phrase "spiritual mapping" defined it as "superimposing our understanding of forces and events in the spiritual domain onto places and circumstances in the material world." The mapping would identify the "social bondages" enslaving the city, such as areas of high drug use and gangs. But it also would show places of a "rampant 'spirit of unbelief,' which tends to be fostered in the area's universities."[12]

While one might consider this mapping to be akin to the data-driven GIS efforts we have today, that was not the case. Spiritual mapping didn't describe a city in granular detail. What it did do was help its practitioners in the minority see more clearly the areas from the 1975 list. A key model for spiritual mapping was the 1989 book *Taking Our Cities for God* by John Dawson, a former staffer with Cunningham's Youth with a Mission. Dawson asked his readers to pray about the "spheres of influence" in a city, listing six areas (excluding media). The city is a "cluster of overlapping institutions," and Satan rules the city by influencing these institutions, marking them "with his own characteristics."[13]

One of the first cities to see the impacts of spiritual mapping was Colorado Springs in the '90s, which then was a growing home to many evangelical missionary organizations. The public radio show *This American Life* profiled the effort there in a September 1997 story: "There's an elaborate program underway involving dozens of churches and thousands of people to pray, not just for those nearby, but to try to fundamentally alter the civic life of their city through prayer." The effort was not evangelistic in any way: "They're not trying to win the hearts and minds of non-Christians by letting them know how much they care about them. In fact, they don't even want the people being prayed for to know that they're being prayed over."[14] While the effort included many churches, *This American Life* focused on the megachurch then run by Ted Haggard, who would go on to become president of the National Association of Evangelicals. (About ten years later he would leave due to a sex scandal.) He claimed that due to this prayer movement the city's crime rate had declined for twelve years straight, though the radio show noted there were other reasons for such a drop.

Spiritual mapping has continued to be used by conservative Christians, especially in politics. The GOP candidate for vice president in 2008, Sarah Palin, was linked to a pastor who not only was a supporter of the seven mountains mandate but also a practitioner of spiritual mapping.[15] This impact continued well into the Trump era. Jennifer Cohn, who has followed the rise of Christian nationalism for the *Bucks County Beacon* in Pennsylvania, profiled a supporter of the seven mountains mandate in the Keystone State in 2023 whose group includes on its website the designation of "state spiritual mapper."[16]

In more recent times, others who have embraced the seven mountains mandate have moved from mapping already existing cities to creating in the twenty-first century their own cities modeled on the medieval concept of Christendom. For example, a 2024 conference in Utah sought to help its supporters build "Christian boroughs" filled with "thick Christian culture." These supporters say their idea comes from "one of the great heroes of the first Christendom," King Alfred the Great in the late 800s.[17] The choice of that figure is no accident. Alfred was praised by Rushdoony in the '90s for insisting God's law rule his realm. The Highland Rim Project, announced in January 2024, is practicing that theology, buying land in Kentucky and Tennessee to "build thick communities that are conducive to a natural, human, and uniquely American way of life."[18] How might these plans seek minority rule? "Thick Christian culture" describes life for all inhabitants under a biblical culture put in place by Christian leaders and formed by Christian institutions, though those leaders may be the minority. Models for such communities already exist in

Hillsdale, Michigan, and Moscow, Idaho, home to two wide-ranging Christian nationalism operations.

Other plans come from a small but growing group that wants to put into power church-like "elders" in cities across the United States. In mainly White evangelical Reformed churches, elders are not only the church's spiritual leaders. They hire and fire, oversee budgets, and sit in judgment in church discipline cases. The group known as City Elders seeks a "Reformation model" that includes "establishing divine order in spiritual and civil governance" in cities and protecting residents from "ungodly individuals rising to positions of power and influence."[19] As of April 2024, there are "city elder councils" in Oklahoma, Arkansas, Texas, Missouri, Kansas, and Virginia, and the group's application for church partners names areas of influence similar to the seven mountains. Frederick Clarkston, an expert on theocratic movements, noted in 2023 that "City Elders has apparently gained remarkable levels of power and influence. Republican candidates and elected officials at all levels speak at their events."[20] For example, Oklahoma governor Kevin Stitt said on X that City Elders is the "backbone" of the Republican Party in his state. For the seven mountains movement, this renewal of Christendom will be the method God uses to spread his goodness and mercy. An Oklahoma state senator who labels himself a supporter of Christian nationalism said in 2024 that such a system of government leads to "the best life for anyone and everyone whether they believe in [God] or not."[21]

Freedom from Tyranny

A God-backed government may be the goal, but the demonic threat of tyranny that Schaeffer described remains what pushes the seven mountains mandate movement today toward antidemocratic violence. Leaders of the movement have taken their cue from Schaeffer on how to respond to modern tyranny, even if it means ignoring some of his words. In his most explicit work on the relationship between Christianity and government, Schaeffer wrote in *A Christian Manifesto* that America was being destroyed by tyranny. In the words of one biographer, "Schaeffer saw only two alternatives for American culture: either society would return to its Christian base, or there would be an imposed order."[22]

While Schaeffer advocated for Christians to resist tyranny, he demurred when asked for specifics. Because Schaeffer was committed theologically to a view of the end-times that predicted social chaos and persecution of Christians, he not only didn't see any form of theocracy arising, but he didn't want it. Yet for the movement today, Schaeffer is a prophet. For example, William Wolfe, author of the 2022 book *The Case for Christian Nationalism*, wrote that the "rapidly metastasizing vision of government" as "the *state*" as an all-controlling entity akin to governments in nondemocratic countries is "at the root of our peril and predicament." He adds in the next line that Schaeffer "saw it coming."[23] Another supporter of Christian nationalism, Pastor Douglas Wilson, who oversees a multi-institutional operation in Moscow, Idaho, wrote that the American government had "declared war on righteousness itself" in the last few decades. Wilson stops short of leading a revolution, though he is clear on what the outcome should be for the "war" he described: "We are simply calling upon God to destroy His enemies. Our first preference is that He destroy them by transforming them into His friends. . . . But if their hearts are hardened, we call upon God to take them out nonetheless."[24]

Because of this type of language, the question of violence is always at the forefront. One reviewer of Wolfe's book put it clearly: "His use of Christian language to defend political violence against a freely elected government should be a bigger scandal than it is: It amounts to a call for holy war against democracy."[25] This rhetoric has a real impact. Christian nationalism was a major theme for those who participated in the 2021 insurrection and its related anti-democracy scheme, "Stop the steal."

Not surprisingly, the mandate movement's spiritual warfare has translated well into Donald Trump's authoritarian political vision. Supporters of the seven mountains mandate have been widely supportive of Trump. And it doesn't matter to the movement that Trump isn't particularly spiritual in practice nor does he act overtly like a Christian. He has been hailed by many as a modern Cyrus, the sixth-century Persian king who ended the Babylonian captivity and is referenced as a figure of Jewish deliverance. As Matthew Taylor points in his 2024 book about the spiritual warfare that supported the 2021 insurrection, "a leader in one of the nonreligion mountains doesn't have to be pious or even necessarily religious to govern according to the kingdom of God. They just have to exert their power in conformity with" the interests of conservative Christians.[26]

As the heir to the seven mountains movement, Charlie Kirk has been a full-throated supporter and defender of Trump. He turned Turning Point into an arm of the Trump 2024 campaign. Kirk and Turning Point support Trump because they share antidemocratic impulses. At times also, Kirk has sounded like Schaeffer about tyranny. Kirk has consistently rehearsed a long list of complaints and cries of tyranny since the early days of the pandemic in 2020 at the end of the first Trump presidency, and not surprisingly, tyranny for Kirk became widespread after Joe Biden was elected. Kirk reformed Turning Point as a resistance group. At a dinner for supporters of a Christian school in Colorado in 2023, Kirk said, "God loves when you defy tyranny for liberty. That is the heart of God. God wants you to reject tyranny if it engages in somebody's life or interferes with their liberty."[27]

Kirk at times has specifically pushed back against people who said they wanted to take up arms against the government. In an exchange at a 2021 Turning Point event in Idaho where Kirk denounced violence against the government, he also directly linked his claims against tyranny with the person who asked him, "When do we get to use the guns?" Kirk said in response that the government was "trying to provoke you and everyone here. They are trying to make you do something that will be violent that will justify a takeover of your freedoms and liberties, the likes of which we have never seen."[28] Despite his pushback in Idaho, there are reasons Kirk got that question. Among those, Turning Point produced episodes for its pop culture show about Ruby Ridge and Waco in October 2021 that frame the leaders of the compounds in those locations raided by the federal government as not merely antigovernment but also defenders of freedom. Kirk also has consistently downplayed the events of January 6, 2021. The Idaho question didn't stall Kirk on tyranny either. He called Trump's arrest in 2023 "a plotted re-founding of America" and a "historic 1776 moment" for Democrats. The only question for Kirk was whether Republicans could stop them.[29]

Laboratories of Antidemocracy

If Trump or another autocrat is the answer to the evils of tyranny at the federal level, the answer from the seven mountains mandate at the state level can be seen in how Turning Point has refashioned the fears of cities grounded in spiritual mapping. But Turning Point doesn't seem interested in mapping those cities for spiritual influence; rather, it seeks to use them to burnish the group's reputation with rural advocates of the seven mountains mandate. Turning Point's plan to Christianize America means spending millions to reshape territory it already owns and spreading from there. If one wants to see how Turning Point is working to conquer the mountain of government, look no further than the "red" states. In another era, conservatives used to say that states were the laboratories of democracy. Now they are easy targets for the antidemocratic mandate movement because conservative enclaves are led by many already primed for further antidemocratic action by the election lies that propelled the 2021 insurrection.

Inspiring action from those states requires Kirk to convince his allies there that their hold on power is threatened. In other words, Kirk and Turning Point are convincing leaders in those states that California and its cities are coming for them. This is why Turning Point has sent its top representatives to the City Elders councils in Oklahoma. Andrew Sypher, Turning Point's director of national field operations (a top general to Kirk), told a City Elders gathering there in February 2024 that he joined Turning Point because he was "tired" of working for conservatives who merely wanted to stay in power. In other words, they were not doing enough to advance the kingdom through their elected position. Sypher said the conservative movement that Turning Point was leading is about "preserving the power of the man on high." "If we keep him in control," this country will continue to be a "bastion of freedom to the world."[30]

Discipleship into Dominion

If Kirk's target audience of "red" states should fear California, there is no better advertiser of that than his mentor into the seven mountains mandate, former California megachurch pastor Rob McCoy.

McCoy was not involved in politics until 2014. That is when he ran and lost a race for California State Assembly. He won a seat on his local city council the next year. He resigned in 2020 in protest of the city's COVID policies. McCoy recently retired from the church he built in Southern California, Godspeak Calvary Chapel. Before he left, he helped to found Turning Point Faith, the arm of Turning Point dedicated to evangelizing into political action White evangelicals through their own churches.

The story McCoy tells of why he got into politics is the story of the failure of the apolitical legacy of his denomination, the Calvary Chapel movement, to shape California politics and culture. In a sermon to a Texas church in January 2020, McCoy recounted the '60s and '70s in the state through the impacts of the hippie movement, political assassinations, and the Vietnam War. He notes how the gospel preaching and new music of Calvary Chapel deliberately avoided politics. Yet now two generations later with "10,000 percent growth" for churches in the Calvary Chapel movement, the state has become morally and financially bankrupt through high taxes, massive debt, and "no-fault" divorce. McCoy said that what is happening in California will get to Texas in a decade.

McCoy doesn't merely make his audience fear a creeping California. In the sermon he consistently refers negatively to the audience's assumption of the "separation of church and state." That's not in the nation's founding documents, McCoy notes. And the Bible itself doesn't say that either. "Every issue of government is in the scriptures," he said. He added the purpose of God's law for all—not just Christians—was for people to live together without an army or police force. McCoy also defended his support for Trump by saying that "God picked" him to be president because American Christians "were not doing anything" to influence the seven mountains. Yet he also adds that "good government" only happens with "good people."[31]

Kirk has parroted time and time again rhetoric from McCoy. For example, during a segment on the radio show of longtime evangelical leader James Dobson in August 2020, Kirk invoked the commonly cited verse from Paul's letter to the church at Rome that says Christians ought to obey the "governing authorities." This would seem illogical in the context of Kirk's litany of complaints about COVID lockdowns and pastors failing to stand up to public health mandates and keep their churches open, but Kirk turned that obedience on its head to argue that "we, the people" are the "sovereign in our country."[32]

This may sound like an exemplary democratic statement. But it is not. In fact, as Kirk used the category, "we the people" stands as a powerful prompt to the White evangelical church. For one, it's clear that the "people" he urges to rise up against tyranny are those Christians. Even then, this may sound like a traditional definition of religious liberty, of a church defying government. But for Kirk it goes beyond civil disobedience. Kirk wants congregants in local churches to claim their authority as "counselor to the king," another concept McCoy passed down to him. Kirk told an audience in 2021 that if the church accepts that role in towns and states across the nations, "all of sudden, all these other problems will start fixing themselves."[33] On the many occasions that Kirk cites this phrase, he usually references individuals in the history of ancient Israel—Daniel in Babylon as the best example—who served a "secular" government leader. But Kirk applies those stories about individuals to the church as a collective influence on the country writ large. This is what the seven mountains mandate has said since its origin.

At the same time, the call for the church to be the nation's sovereign also means for Kirk that it can rebel against the government. In one sense, Kirk is saying that Christians as individuals and as a collective can ignore government authority by claiming freedom from it (or actually, authority over it). They can ignore any law, ordinance, or even policy they find tyrannical. Yet on the other hand Kirk promotes his desire for those same Christians to rule the government. Practically, Kirk calls for Christians in "blue" states to ignore government authority and calls for Christians in "red" states to claim it. If one frames such illogic in terms of the debate over federalism—the role of national government versus the states—one steps very clearly toward Greene's national divorce.

Tracing a Line

McCoy got into politics because of the influence of an evangelical network builder named David Lane, who has spent his life getting pastors like McCoy on ballots. He has done that mainly through his American Renewal Project. Lane told the Christian Broadcasting Network in 2019, "We're going to turn America back to [God] and re-establish a Christian culture."[34] McCoy and Lane share California as a foil in their Christian nationalism rhetoric. Kirk has been a speaker at Lane's events in California and has parroted Lane in the same way he has parroted McCoy. Both have used the mantra that the most important thing is spreading the gospel, and "preserving the liberty to win people to Christ is the second most important thing."[35]

While Lane may sound like a supporter of democracy, his Christian nationalism rhetoric has become more despondent about democracy as a method for the spiritual and political renewal of America. And he shows where Kirk is headed. Frederick Clarkson's 2014 profile of Lane asserted that Lane's "apparent lack of confidence that the Christian Right's efforts to establish theocratic governance can succeed by using the tools of democracy epitomizes the idea that martyrdom and elections are not mutually exclusive, and that horrific confrontations lie ahead." Clarkson noted that even the biblical characters Lane invokes and the way he invokes them isn't done to seek religious revival or advance a legislative agenda. It's done to make more militant his theocratic vision.[36]

More than a decade has passed since that analysis, and the militancy has only skyrocketed, now propelled by the millions from Turning Point. This is quite a departure from Kirk's motives at the time of Turning Point's founding, when he described himself as having libertarian leanings and promoted policies like cutting the federal deficit and paying off the growing national debt. In 2019—before Kirk met McCoy and moved toward Christian nationalism—the mission statement of Turning Point was to "promote the principles of freedom, free markets, and limited government," all libertarian if not also conservative causes. By 2024, that mission had been updated. According to a post on X, Turning Point now wants to "restore traditional American values like patriotism, respect for life, liberty, family, and fiscal responsibility." The erasure of "limited government" is important to note. It's not that Kirk has denounced it. It's that Kirk has found a different source of authority for government: the church. That ideology may shrink the federal government's budget. But it also may strengthen the governmental role for the church in American life.

It is ironic that in the '60s Protestants feared a Catholic president because they assumed he would be under the power of the pope. An America working under biblical government as described by the seven mountains mandate looks more like the movie *Footloose*, where pastors and other Christians rule on local and state legislative bodies, perhaps excising the federal government from the equation. The only deliberation will be over minute theological issues. As "counselor to the king," a dominion-minded American Christian minority would implicitly and explicitly decide through the counsel of the church (through its traditions, texts, and interpreters) which values, laws, and policies should be in place throughout America.

What might that mean for religious freedom? During a 2020 episode of *The Charlie Kirk Show*, McCoy has said he didn't turn Kirk toward a theocracy, because America is a "pluralistic society."[37] But that one nod to pluralism is hardly repeated at all by McCoy, and it's not found in the history of the seven mountains movement. As Bruce Barron, one of the earliest scholars to write about the seven mountains mandate, put in his 1992 book, there is no tolerance of religious pluralism in the kind of Christian society envisioned by Rushdoony and his lineage. In their view, the First Amendment "barred religious establishment only at the federal level, not the state level." And "since different religions promote irreconcilable concepts of law, total religious toleration is 'neither possible nor desirable.'"[38]

It's clear that Kirk and his followers in the mandate movement see democracy when they win, tyranny when they lose. That is, they don't offer their consent as governed parties to any electoral or policy loss to the other side. And it is also clear if given power, those who support the mandate want to remove the power of consent from those unworthy in their eyes to give it. In his book *The Case for Christian Nationalism*, Wolfe argued that the consent of the governed is moot for non-Christians in a Christian state: "The issue here centers on whether a Christian minority can establish a political state over the whole without the positive consent of the whole. I affirm they can. . . . The Christian's posture toward the earth ought to be that it is ours, not theirs, for we are co-heirs in Christ."[39] But a democracy demands you can't love your country only when you win, as Joe Biden said many times throughout his presidency. Kirk says that "if there is any hope" for the United States, "that hope is the church." Sadly, what Kirk and Turning Point's sweeping plan for government actually does is dash hope for both.

Chapter Three

Biblical Citizenship

The Mountain of Religion

Sitting on the floor of the U.S. Capitol on January 6, 2021, at times coughing into a black-and-white scarf due to what seems like smoke in the building, a thin, bearded White man in his thirties named Tyler Ethridge put himself live on the internet.

Like many there that day, Ethridge denounced the "stolen election." He said the time for mere words was over. Then he said, "I'm probably going to lose my job as a pastor after this."

Ethridge was right. Days later the Florida church where he had been a youth pastor for about a year announced on its Facebook page he no longer worked there.

More than eighteen months later he was arrested. The Department of Justice said in a statement about his arrest that before entering the building, Ethridge "climbed a media scaffolding and exhorted the crowd to keep fighting" as police attempted to clear the crowd. The DOJ said Ethridge then joined a group of people staring down a line of police in riot gear between the Rotunda and the Senate chamber. He stayed in the building for about half an hour. In 2024 he was sentenced to seven months in federal prison and was released from prison in January 2025 after President Trump's mass pardons on Inauguration Day for those involved in the insurrection.

What would drive a pastor to be part of an insurrection?[1]

The 2021 riot was not merely the effect of lies about the 2020 election, but the decades-long influence of the seven mountains mandate. The mountain of religion is central to the rise of the mandate movement. One might wonder why religion is included among the mountains at all. It perhaps should go without saying that Christians already run the church. But for the supporters of the seven mountains movement, the church is included in the powerful places controlled by Satan. The movement wants to purify the church from demonic influences, make it more willing to act as the nation's moral enforcer, and make it more militant in that action. This claim was born in traditionally White churches within American evangelicalism, whose conservative theology often saw mainline denominations as culturally corrupt and historic Black churches as theologically suspect. This is why the seven mountains plan is "a form of religious privilege—for their kind of religion," as Katherine Stewart said in her book on Christian nationalism.[2]

A Worldview and Its Mandate

That privilege is grounded in a biblical worldview that brings a very specific interpretation of the Bible and Christian faith to bear on our national cultural features. Ethridge embodies the worldview he received at Charis Bible College in Colorado, founded by Andrew Wommack, an advocate of the seven mountains mandate. In their third year, students at Charis choose among seven areas of concentration that mirror the seven mountains: church ministry, business, entertainment, and so forth. Ethridge nodded to the impact of worldview in his video from the Capitol. The actions that day by the insurrectionist mob may not have been morally right, Ethridge said, but they were the actions needed to meet the moment: "This is what pastors need to do. . . . Christians, we need to infiltrate every area of society like this. Every area of society, like this. Peacefully. But if it takes a little bit of aggression to barge through the walls that Satan separates us from the culture, it's time for the body of Christ to infiltrate the culture."

In the late nineteenth and early twentieth centuries, the Dutch theologian Abraham Kuyper saw the need for a Christian "life-view" to answer the rise of modernism. He presented the biblical worldview "as a total framework of biblical thought" and applied its "implications in the areas of religion, politics, science, and art."³ In the '40s Carl Henry, the first editor of the long-respected evangelical publication *Christianity Today* and author of often-cited books in evangelical cultural thinking and theology, promoted the idea of a Christian worldview to American evangelicalism. Francis Schaeffer framed such a worldview as that which would stand against any interrogation. He saw Christianity as a system of truth, "the only system that will stand up to all the questions that are presented to us as we face the reality of existence." Schaeffer's acolytes in the '80s formed the Coalition on Revival and created a set of "worldview" documents that laid out biblical principles for more than fifteen spheres of human life, including many of the seven mountains but also medicine, law, and "helping the hurting," among others.⁴

A Shift to Spiritual Warfare

If Schaeffer wanted the biblical worldview to stand up to intellectual assault, the mandate movement after his death in 1984 wanted the worldview to win. That victory started in a battle against the church. For decades, advocates of the mandate movement have claimed the American church—both its pastors and congregants—have not done enough to stem the tide of moral and spiritual decay in the nation. The church was labeled complacent, indifferent, or timid. In a 1988 sermon, a South Florida megachurch pastor with a national television platform proclaimed the church was failing in its role. The nation's decay can't be pinned on the "humanists" or "secularists" in America, the founder of Coral Ridge Ministries, D. James Kennedy, said. The church "as a whole" hasn't done its job discipling the nation. "We have failed to obey the Great Commission in this country as a whole. We have failed to obey the Cultural Mandate to be involved in every sphere of activity. We have retreated from politics, government, the media, and higher education, and we have left it to nonbelievers. We have failed to fulfill our responsibilities as citizens."⁵

The seven mountains movement had turned the cultural mandate into a cultural war. That war came by pushing from the margins of

American Christianity into wider usage the concept of spiritual warfare. By the turn of the millennium, the person credited with renewing the movement, Lance Wallnau, saw the war in clear militant terms. While he mentioned prayer and evangelism as methods for societal change, in a 2005 book Wallnau framed his ideas around a greater "ideological conflict" that the seven "mind molders" have created. That conflict is "in fact a cultural war" that has become "incendiary" since 2000. Wallnau pits Satan offering Jesus the kingdoms of the world against "believers" who take it back "by force."[6] Here he cites Mark 11:12, but that is an error. Wallnau clearly meant Matthew 11:12, in which Jesus describes the frenzy of people coming to see him and John the Baptist before him. Such is compared to those who might take a city, "and the violent take it by force." One scholar who has studied Wallnau's imagery said his 2005 claim "brought with it a whole new provocation to conquest and strategy for battle."[7] By 2009, seven mountains advocate and self-described "social reformer" Johnny Enlow offered a justification of cultural dominion. Enlow made clear that the command to Christians was not merely to "rescue souls" but also to "destroy the devil's works—his works in government, in the media, in educational institutions, in Hollywood, in Wall Street, in families, *and in the religious landscape.*"[8]

Empowered Pastors

As heir to this lineage, Charlie Kirk and Turning Point have promoted a biblical worldview that can "design and construct an entire society," as he told the Texas Youth Summit in a 2023 speech entitled "Fake Worldviews, and the True One."[9] Kirk laments a worldview crisis among evangelicals, citing a lack of adherence to eight categories of beliefs and behaviors defined by the Barna Research Group, a long-standing survey organization friendly to evangelicals. In 2024, Barna suggested that—according to its own criteria—only 4 percent of American adults hold a biblical worldview. And that "will drop another two points within the next 15 years, unless some dramatic and unusually effective spiritual renewal event occurs."[10]

That call to action is the unifying factor for Kirk and Turning Point as they implement their version of an old playbook. The first step is to empower allied pastors. Kirk's call to pastors was steeled in him during the COVID pandemic when he claimed that the move by state and local governments to limit large gatherings in the spring of 2020 was nothing less than tyranny "based on a lie." But Kirk was aghast when he saw only a few churches refusing to obey. The large majority of pastors cowered and their people suffered, he said. He called into action his minority of allies: "The totalitarianism they're trying to implement in America . . . must go through the church first."[11]

Emphasis on the minority is part of the strategy. Turning Point uses some of the same rhetoric to appeal to pastors that made it successful with its original minority, conservative young adults. But there are also noticeable differences in approach. Turning Point's celebrity-fed student summits include popular musical artists, "meet and greets" with politicians and conservative media figures, and a mantra of "Life, Liberty, and the Pursuit to Party!" In stark contrast, Turning Point's pastor summits are not glitzy and glamorous. They are likely to take place in small hotel ballrooms with intimate lighting, and with less emphasis on celebrities (though special guests have included Michael Oher, former NFL star and subject of the movie *The Blind Side*). With fewer than one thousand attendees, the summits are small compared to Turning Point's youth-oriented events. But the smallness matters. It allows Turning Point to raise even more the stakes of the mountain of religion by comparing its group of allies to the small band of rebels that signed the Declaration of Independence. As Kirk told the 2023 summit, the pastors gathered there had to get "liberty" right because if they didn't, they would be preaching from prison.

Getting liberty right, to leaders of the seven mountains mandate movement including Kirk, means advancing myths about American history. Turning Point has called its biblical worldview "a providential worldview" because of a belief in how divine providence not only led America to be founded as a Christian nation but also how the Lord brings into being "blessings" for individuals in the nation.[12] Turning Point offers pastors training in how to preach about the Constitution and the biblical worldview, offering sermon resources with suggested outlines and polished graphics for worship screens and social media.

Kirk has said not enough Christians are taking action to save America because they "do not know prior courageous action" by those in the nation's history.[13] He has often repeated debunked claims about colonial American history, featuring the misinterpretations long taught by the seven mountains mandate movement's favorite "historian," David Barton.

A Turning Point pastor-summit speaker makes clear what the organization's version of pastoral courage looks like in practice: A former offensive lineman for the Chicago Bears, Oklahoma pastor Paul Blair runs a network of churches mainly in the Sooner State and Florida that trains pastors "to think Biblically in EVERY area of life."[14] Blair frames the colonial era as the unification of Christians against a British king who wanted to limit religious freedom and install a "state church." And the "backbone" of the move to independence was a group of "patriot pastors," a reference to a myth spread by Kirk and Barton among others. Blair's group says that preachers have "led in the fight against every social ill in America, whether that be slavery, discrimination, suffrage, liquor, abortion, etc."[15] It's not surprising then that Blair's group was named as part of a "remnant alliance" aiming to take over school boards in Texas in 2024.[16] He also appeared on Kirk's podcast in May 2023 to spread conspiracy theories about a "global digital currency."[17]

Kirk and Turning Point have a word for those pastors who don't join them: cowards. While Kirk says that "cowards can be turned," he has also said that some pastors are not merely afraid to speak "truth" but that they don't know what it is. He has said he doesn't believe some of them are Christians at all.[18] Kirk told a conservative media site in 2023 that "the vast majority of churches are cowardly. . . . They're just kind of a shell of what they could be."[19]

Empowered Prophets

Pastors are not the only group of religious leaders the seven mountains movement wants to motivate, and Turning Point has turned to this other group too. The other audience is leaders in a growing movement that scholar Matthew Taylor writes about in his 2024 book titled, fittingly, *The Violent Take It by Force*. These leaders are apostles "mobilizing spiritual warfare campaigns to target whole nations for deliverance and salvation."[20] The role of apostles in Christianity goes back to its earliest days, as the original disciples were given that title. To many noncharismatic Protestants, the role ended during that era. But for charismatics, the role of apostle is as needed today as it was then. The university founded by Peter Wagner, one of the forefathers of the seven mountains movement, offers a master's degree in "apostolic leadership," which trains students in the seven mountains mandate so they can bring revival and reformation and then cultural transformation to nations.[21]

Amid all speakers at Turning Point's pastor summits, one name stands out as an exemplar of Turning Point's apostolic strategy. He is one of the key leaders in the growing global movement Taylor has charted known as the New Apostolic Reformation: Ché Ahn. His network of churches, Harvest International, spans seventy nations. Ahn is also a major part of the seven mountains mandate movement. Ahn spoke at the 2023 Turning Point pastor summit on a panel with one of his acolytes, singer and Turning Point partner Sean Feucht. Ahn envisioned a "revival and reformation" of the church and nation, echoing Wagner University.[22] In a 2009 book, Ahn said such a reformation would come through the combination of teaching people "a basic Judeo-Christian worldview" and "the right structures" that would eliminate systemic issues like poverty.[23] This is the cultural mandate.

Ahn is fiercely antigovernment—or more precisely, government that conflicts with his theology. He repeatedly emphasized that in an October 2023 sermon where he specifically cited his own church's refusal to obey California pandemic policies. He likened the act of protest to the work of the German pastor Dietrich Bonhoeffer, who was killed by the Nazis near the end of World War II for participating in a plot to assassinate Hitler. Like Kirk, Ahn played a key role in the Trump plan to overturn the 2020 election. He appeared at a rally on January 5, 2021—one day before the Capitol insurrection—where he proclaimed that Trump would stay in power and that Christians would "rule and reign through President Trump and under the lordship of Jesus Christ."[24] Ahn made a similar decree right before Trump's 2024 win.

While Turning Point promotes apostles, Kirk's status amid them is a fine example of how Kirk downplays the more extreme parts of the seven mountains movement while simultaneously promoting it. Kirk is clearly an heir to these apostles by ideology. If he becomes an heir by identification, his power will only rise. But neither he nor any person within Wagner's network has claimed that title for him—yet.

That doesn't mean what he is doing doesn't already fit Wagner's definitions. Wagner's group says a key piece of evidence for recognizing an apostle is that they are a "primary point person of a network, a movement, a major thought leader, or influencer with a substantial following." As Turning Point strives to organize efforts for all seven mountains, Kirk's work is not limited to one sphere. And he certainly is an influencer. There is an obvious reason Kirk hasn't taken on the titles of those who advocated the seven mountains mandate before him: The title "apostle" can sound more than strange not only to large segments of evangelicalism but also to the larger social and cultural conservative world. As Kirk seeks to expand his empire and that of the mandate movement, he knows his forefathers can only get him so far.

Empowered Churches

As part of their plan to conquer the mountain of religion, Kirk and Turning Point want to change evangelical institutions. They have turned the powerful (though shrinking) Southern Baptist Convention to the seven mountains. The convention has a long history of promoting religious freedom. But in recent years the convention's National Day of Prayer has been centered on "seven centers of influence in America."[25] That occurred during the tenure of Ronnie Floyd, once a megachurch pastor in Arkansas and then CEO of the Southern Baptist Convention from 2019 to 2021. He was a speaker at the 2023 Turning Point pastor summit. That invitation likely was a result of Kirk and Turning Point building a relationship with the Conservative Baptist Network, a far-right faction in the denomination. Kirk and Turning Point hosted a breakfast for members of that group (through a $50,000 donation) in 2022 near the denomination's annual convention in Anaheim, California.[26] Allies of the group have repeated Kirk's rhetoric about the role of the church against government, saying that disobedience to tyrants is biblical.

As they work to persuade evangelical leaders, Turning Point is also aiming to convince congregants. It is radicalizing civic training in evangelical churches, resurrecting "biblical citizenship" to put the civil war of politics directly in the pew. These trainings have roots in the origins of the seven mountains mandate movement. In his 1986 book about the areas of cultural influence, Bill Bright highlights a congregation in Oregon that had begun teaching a citizenship class during its adult Sunday school time, encouraging participation in all levels of government by church members. The pastor told Bright that while God "created government," Christians had neglected "developing biblical perspectives" on it.[27] (Not surprisingly, that church was also home to Stu Weber, who wrote the book *Tender Warriors*, which started the evangelical push about biblical manhood in the '90s. See chapter 4 on the mountain of family.)

For its trainings, Turning Point has partnered with a group called Patriot Academy. Led by former Texas legislator Rick Green, Patriot Academy partners with David Barton to teach Barton's Constitution Alive! curriculum. The academy also includes a class that combines constitutional curriculum with "intense, combat-focused pistol training."[28] Patriot Academy, Green, Barton, and Kirk were part of a "biblical citizenship barnstorming tour" during runoff elections in Georgia in 2020.

In the summer of 2024, Turning Point and Patriot Academy also partnered on a series of trainings for teens and young adults called Leadership Congress. The call for attendees framed the training as part of the seven mountains movement (plus one): "We are looking for men and women who are ready to influence and lead across all areas of the culture—family, religion, education, media, entertainment, business, government, and technology." The training is designed to mimic the work of legislative bodies, and participants were trained through "floor sessions" where bills were introduced and voted on. The sessions took place in the legislative chambers of state governments.

The training also had a clear religious element, not merely because of sessions on God's purpose for government. Each day began with a devotional and ended with "fellowship," a term often used in Christian settings for social gatherings. Turning Point also refashions similar evangelical terms for the seven mountains agenda. In a video promoting Turning Point's biblical citizenship course, megachurch pastor Jack Hibbs defines citizenship as a form of "stewardship," a term commonly used by evangelicals when they speak of personal finances and the environment. Good stewards will be rewarded for their individual management of resources. But the seven mountains movement sees political stewardship as part of biblical citizenship, broadening that individual judgment to include nations. From this perspective, America is a Christian nation to be judged on whether it has lived out its divinely mandated identity. This also means individual Christians will be judged on how they helped maintain or rebirth America as a Christian nation.

Antidemocratic Civic Action

It may not be surprising to learn that the Oregon church Bright wrote about, Good Shepherd Community Church in Boring, still exists and lists "biblical citizenship" as part of its values and cites a verse commonly used by the supporters of the seven mountains mandate: "But seek the welfare of the city where I have sent you into exile, and pray to the LORD on its behalf, for in its welfare you will find your welfare" (Jeremiah 29:7). Kirk referenced that same verse when he announced in 2021 the creation of Freedom Square, a monthly event for promoting Christian nationalism centered in Dream City Church in Phoenix. But Kirk changes the tone of the verse by saying *"demand* the welfare" (emphasis mine), which is not found in any English translation, and as one scholar of the text notes, "demand" in the context of those exiles—who had no power—is absurd.[29]

Kirk and allies see in this verse an aggressive imperative that if followed by Christians will create "the separation of sheep and goat nations," where the former are praised and protected by a returning Jesus. This is a reference to Matthew 25, though the seven mountains mandate website that cites it only quotes to verse 34, thus excluding the criteria Jesus gives for discerning sheep from goats.[30] This kind of rhetoric poisons the civic training that would be a sign of a healthy democracy if it was not attached to the radicalism of Christian nationalism. Reflecting this growing intensity, conservative media commentator Eric Metaxas told the 2023 Turning Point pastor summit that "what you preach and what you say matters a thousand times more than it did ten years ago or twenty years ago."[31]

If dominion is the theological principle that unites the movement, then the political principle is "participatory antidemocracy." Participatory antidemocracy is a term coined by a scholar of fascism, Joseph Fronczak, in a 2018 article where he described a strikebreaker effort in the 1930s that turned "a management-labor dispute into an ideological struggle waged throughout the entire social theater, politicizing the public."[32] Fronczak compared this to the "ready-for-a-fight" movement in the 2010s known as the Tea Party (where, not coincidentally, Kirk got his start).[33]

Kirk exemplified this participatory antidemocracy with his call to action in the lead-up to the 2024 presidential election: "I want to make sure we all make a commitment that if this election doesn't go our way, the next day we'd fight." Many attendees applauded, though Kirk derided it as "golf applause" because he questioned their commitment. Kirk then compared Christians who didn't want to "fight" after an election loss to those who didn't want to fight for liberty in 1776 once the winter came. Kirk called such people "sunshine patriots," a reference to the second sentence of a famous pamphlet by Thomas Paine, one of the authors who helped spur the colonists to revolution. Paine wrote in November 1776, "THESE are the times that try men's souls. The summer soldier and the sunshine patriot will, in this crisis, shrink from the service of their country; but he that stands by it now, deserves the love and thanks of man and woman." Days later George Washington read the pamphlet to his troops before they made the fateful crossing of the Delaware River in December, and likewise, Kirk hoped to spur his followers to similarly valiant action, if necessary. As Paine's third sentence declares, "Tyranny, like hell, is not easily conquered."

The risk of losing at the ballot box seems to be part of why Kirk often recoils at saying America is a democracy and instead demands it be known as a republic. He held to this mythical difference even before turning to Christian nationalism, but it is a false dichotomy. The United States is both. And with Trump's victory in 2024, Kirk won't turn away from promoting the idea of an American republic. That's because a republic promotes certain values—those found, according to Kirk and his allies, in natural law and the Bible.

Kirk's Christian republic will use democracy to initially assert itself. Peter Wagner wrote in 2008 that "the best form of human government before Jesus returns is not theocracy, but democracy." That may sound strange from an early leader in the dominion movement. But in rejecting "an imagined 'ecclesiocracy' in which the Church would rule," Wagner said, the "rules of the democratic game" can open the doors for Christians to rule through "positions of leadership influential enough to shape the whole nation from top to bottom." This is why Wagner's ideal for success is when a transformed society happens "simultaneously" on all mountains.[34]

Kirk adds to that ideal an appeal to undermine the very Constitution he claims to honor. Kirk said in 2022 that the U.S. Constitution is only fit for a moral and religious people, paraphrasing a 1798 letter written by John Adams.[35] That letter was Adams's justification to the Massachusetts militia for the empowering of a Christian government against the same kind of moral rot Kirk and the seven mountains mandate movement fear today. One historian called the justification by Adams "an extraconstitutional means of controlling the kinds of unbridled human passions that, in Adams' view, the Constitution alone could not control."[36] Many experts think Trump is the next one to try to implement that extraconstitutional control. For Kirk, the church is the nation's moral guardian and Trump is a long-sought arm of the Lord.

A Kingdom Democracy

This is made clear by Ché Ahn, who told a January 5, 2021, rally that the church has the answers to the problems of society: "We can't just wait for the government—you are [God's] *ekklesia*, you are his legislative body of the Kingdom of God and you need to be involved."[37] *Ekklesia* is a Greek term meaning "assembly" or "gathering" and is often translated as "church" in English-language Bibles. In ancient

Athens it was the gathering of citizens who debated policy and use of power. Ahn and others in the mandate movement say that Jesus called his church *ekklesia* (most famously in Matthew 16:18) to give it the same power. One early adopter in the mandate movement of this concept argued that "when the Roman Empire would conquer new territory," it "would send some of their Roman citizens to be the local *ekklesia*, as in governing assembly, and thereby impose the culture of Rome on the new territory."[38] As another supporter of the idea notes, "Just as the Athenian *ekklesia* ruled in matters of law, business, society, customs, culture, and judicial matters, God expects the Church to exert its spiritual influence in every arena of the society in which it exists."[39]

The church as *ekklesia* is a theological concept with enormous impact in practice. Greg Hood, the founder of a training center for advocates of the seven mountains movement known as Kingdom University, described in 2023 a dream he had in which God revealed to him that the day Congress counted the Electoral College votes in 2021—January 6—began a "great lie" that powers a "cycle of overthrowing this nation," and that in response, he should "deploy the Ekklesia." Hood compared the leaders in the church today to pastors who worked during the American Revolution, "men that would pull their pistols out and lay them on the pulpit and preach their message and holster them again and take their robes off and under that robe would be a continental uniform." To "deploy the *ekklesia*" today meant to see the church as a "command center" to aid the "assignment" of every city and state "to bring forth the kingdom of God like we've never seen it on the earth before."[40]

Kirk has likened *ekklesia* to a "city council meeting."[41] To compare this concept to a democratically elected body may seem to give it an aura of legitimacy, but the seven mountains movement doesn't want a city council at all. It wants the church to act as such, its unelected leaders governing the city. In other words, the secular city council will not be outvoted. They will be merely outed and replaced. One Turning Point pastors' summit speaker, the president of a group that seeks to redefine religious liberty laws, described such an outing this way: "Every person needs to go in their own community and say, 'Why don't we have prayer at the school board meeting? Why don't we have a Nativity scene? . . . It's just a matter of if we're willing to take the ground or not. This is us going on offense and they can't stop us. We just have to move."[42] The belief, as scholar Matthew Taylor describes it, is that God "[put] Christians in charge of the earth in the spiritual realm, an authority they can use to 'legislate'—that is, change reality—in the natural realm."[43] This kind of talk often raises fears of theocracy. Whatever label one wants to use, the plan is a rule by Christians and Christianity. Such a government system would privilege Christianity even if the majority are not Christians.

The Question of Religious Liberty

Clearly the seven mountains movement poses a threat to democracy. It is also a specific threat to the religious pluralism of modern America. Where do the two other major monotheistic religions fit into the seven mountains plan?

There has been a long debate among evangelicals about Israel (both ancient and modern), its relationship to America, and the endtimes. One group, called "dispensationalists," sees a clear distinction between Israel and the church, so much that Christians are not bound by laws as laid out in the Jewish scriptures and that God's promises to the biblical Israel must be fulfilled with the modern nation of Israel. In this view, the founding of Israel was a cosmically significant event that "meant the world's final events would begin to unfold within a generation."[44]

Dispensationalist views have all but disappeared among evangelical seminaries and theologians. Not coincidentally, many dispensationalists did not support and actively criticized early forms of the seven mountains movement in the '70s and '80s. Dispensationalist author Hal Lindsey, whose novels fictionalized the end of the world, feared that seeing the United States as the new chosen nation of God would demean promises made to the nation of Israel and in turn demean Jews, furthering prejudice and hate. Lindsey warned Christians to "not sit idly by while a system of prophetic interpretation that historically furnished the philosophical basis for anti-Semitism infects the Church again."[45]

There is no question that Kirk and Turning Point are strong supporters of the nation of Israel. Turning Point has hosted leadership summits for young Jewish students since 2019. It has also sent students to Israel for educational trips, promoted Israel in its educational materials, and promoted "Jewish thought-leaders," including Dennis Prager, a mentor to Kirk.[46] Kirk also repeats verses in Jewish scriptures cited by others who defend supporting modern Israel. But Kirk has repeatedly said at Turning Point's pastor summits that he doesn't want his audience to divide over the end-times. This echoes other groups in the past who have pursued forms of Christian nationalism. For example, in the '80s, the Coalition on Revival had a "non-quarreling policy" about the end-times, which pushed divided camps to pursue political change together.[47]

Despite its support of Israel, Turning Point has also spread anti-Semitism.[48] In 2022, Kirk spread a conspiracy theory linked to the World Economic Forum called the Great Reset (see chapter 6 on media). The conspiracy is grounded in anti-Semitic tropes about Jews running global finances. But the reset goes beyond the economy. Kirk says its goal is to erase Western values and biblical values, what are often termed "Judeo-Christian values." As historians have noted, Judeo-Christian is a conjured phrase used by those who want not only to stamp the nation's history and future as Christian but also to elide the first religion in the phrase.[49]

That phrase also excludes the third major monotheistic religion, Islam. The seven mountains movement is distinctively Christian, primarily Protestant. But it has differing opinions about Islam. One of the earliest leaders in the mandate movement, Peter Wagner, was not theologically supportive of Islam, but he wanted the religion to have freedom like Christianity. He supported the freedom to open mosques, especially in the early years after the 2001 terror acts. He told NPR in 2011 that he is sorry that "some radicals speak up strongly against having a mosque in their neighborhood, and I don't think that's patriotism. I think America needs to make room for liberty."[50] But other advocates of the seven mountains mandate have not had the same affirming relationship toward Islam.[51] There have been incidents of Turning Point staff degrading Islam. While Kirk personally supported a Muslim who ran for Congress in Arizona in 2024 who has spent years denouncing "political Islam" or Islamic states, Kirk has suggested that "Islamic migrants entering the West" want to undermine its virtues.[52]

When Kirk speaks of religious freedom, he hardly ever mentions other religions outside Protestant sects. He also says that the founders' definition of religious freedom is to be understood in the context of most founders being Christians. Using that myth, Kirk then claims the framers understood the clause in the Constitution barring the national establishment of a religion to mean that the government would not choose favorites among Protestant sects. He told a version of this to the conservative talk show host Kirk Cameron in 2022: "This was actually not that religion has no place in government but it was a promise to every single strain of Protestant tradition in the colonial times that [America] was not going to become an Anglican or Episcopalian or Quaker or Presbyterian or Lutheran country, that every single denomination would be respected."[53] The implication here is that, at the very least, a nation under the rule of the seven mountains mandate would be generally Protestant.

Another reason the seven mountains movement is dangerous to religious pluralism is that its mandate pushes societal or cultural reformation as a steppingstone to spiritual revival. For example, Kirk claims that America's laws as modeled from Christian scriptures should guide us all toward the spiritual freedom from sin offered by God through Christianity. As Kirk told a church named Cross Assembly in North Carolina in 2020, those who believe in values like freedom and liberty but don't know Jesus as their savior want to "go upstream" and find the "source" of those values.[54] How they discover that source is often left open to interpretation by Turning Point and other allies of the seven mountains movement. In his book about seeing Christian nationalism as a mission field, Arizona pastor Caleb Campbell recounts a meeting with a Turning Point employee who said she "met Jesus" at a Turning Point event.[55] This kind of path from mandate to missiology is what makes Christian nationalism scholar Matthew Taylor say the seven mountains movement has crossed over "from religious freedom to Christian supremacy" and "represents a deeply antidemocratic agenda."[56]

The seven mountains mandate plan for America aims to end the reign of the unbridled demon atop all our national cultural institutions. The White evangelical church in that plan is to be a command center for such warfare, spiritual or otherwise. The strategy is the Christian worldview. And that requires a citizenship beyond the Constitution. It requires a biblical one. Who gets to be a citizen in such a society? And what democratic institutions will be available for pluralism to be practiced? The answers have come into sharp relief as Turning Point has begun to enforce this worldview.

Chapter Four

The Masculine Heart and the Feminine Mystique

The Mountain of Family

The date was July 23, 2023. The Walmart in Hastings, Nebraska, was the trap.

Two Turning Point staffers working with its "exposing evil" media unit called Frontlines CSU (child safety unit) had set up a meeting with a twenty-three-year-old Nebraskan named Chris whom they had been communicating with under the guise of being a twelve-year-old girl.

Their goal: to catch a predator.

But Turning Point had no idea what it was doing. And the scheme blew up in their face.

The Turning Point staffer leading the effort, Kalen D'Almeida, would go on to be arrested and enter a pretrial diversion program later that year for assaulting another of his targets, an Arizona State University professor (see chapter 1). D'Almeida and Turning Point told Hastings police that they had started communicating with Chris in February. They had recordings and chat logs of what they said were sexually explicit conversations between their decoy and Chris. A nearly eight-minute video by Frontlines, styled with red lights in a dark studio set with D'Almeida "anchoring" the exposé, said Chris had been recently identifying as a transgender female. Chris told the Frontlines team that surgery was scheduled for the coming fall.

Now Chris, wearing blue pants and a tight-fitting T-shirt that spelled "love" on several lines and in "the pride rainbow color scheme," as Frontlines called it, was standing in the girls' clothing section ready to meet in person.

Instead, D'Almeida confronted Chris, ambush style, while a Turning Point staffer recorded the encounter. Like Chris Hansen on the NBC show *To Catch a Predator* that ran from 2004 to 2008, D'Almeida tried to entice Chris to chat. But very quickly Chris became visibly angry and walked away. D'Almeida and his camera operator followed. Chris moved quickly through the store and then through the sliding doors of the main entrance and into a tan sedan, all the while trying to get the Turning Point crew to stop following. The crew followed anyway, yelling, "That's what you did," after recounting some of the things from the conversations.

Eventually Chris got into a car. D'Almeida banged on the driver's window with his knuckles as the car backed up. In a rush to get away, Chris backed into a blue truck. Chris took off anyway but eventually was tracked down by police at a gas station a few miles away.

Police interviewed Chris and the Turning Point staff and taught D'Almeida a quick lesson in Nebraska law. While Chris was cited for the hit and run, there were no sex crime charges because in Nebraska only law enforcement is allowed to be a decoy. In addition, rather than skillfully waiting for the target to initiate predatory contact, the Turning Point decoy began the communication with Chris, restarted communication after Chris cut off communication, and asked Chris to meet. Hastings police said in a statement posted to its Facebook page after Frontlines went public with its ambush that "it is disappointing" Frontlines and Turning Point didn't inform police ahead of time: "Due to their lack of understanding regarding Nebraska Laws [*sic*] and processes, they have obtained information that cannot legitimately be used by law enforcement to further an investigation or criminal prosecution with this incident."[1]

Despite these errors, Turning Point flooded social media with its ambush video, which went viral with millions of views. Charlie Kirk hosted the Frontlines team on his national radio show. Despite numerous and ongoing headlines of police using decoys in chat rooms to arrest unsuspecting people, Kirk questioned police behavior in this case because of the transgender element. Police had explained why it couldn't use any of the recordings Frontlines had, but Kirk asked D'Almeida on that September show, "Do you think that the local law enforcement in Hastings is afraid to proceed because this person is trans?" D'Almeida said it was a "possibility" because "people are afraid to act against any class of protected people."[2]

Enforcing the Family Code

D'Almeida told Kirk on his radio show that what Turning Point did in its Nebraska "raid on the transgender pedophile," everyone should do: "We want to do our part to protect children, and we know how to do it. We should be doing it. Everyone should be doing it."[3] The "transgender pedophile" has joined a long list of villains targeted by evangelical preachers, politicians, and groups associated with the seven mountains mandate. And all stories of villains also need heroes. Turning Point framed itself as the hero in its quest to conquer the mountain of family: "Transgender sex perverts have become the mascots and high priests of America's ruling regime, but they are still predators, and if police won't stop them, then Turning Point will."[4]

Turning Point bills itself as a form of cultural law enforcement, and as with reclaiming the education mountain, such enforcement does not merely mean persuasion but punishment. To conquer the mountain of family, Turning Point as an ally with the larger Christian nationalism movement aims to erase from our national identity those who don't follow its moral code. Michael Knowles, a Turning Point campus speaker who headlines his own *Daily Wire* show, told an audience at a conservative conference in 2023 that "transgenderism" should be completely eradicated from public life. The crowd erupted in applause. Knowles has been an open supporter of Christian nationalism, saying that America is "a Christian country. Most people are Christian. It's just a Christian country. There's no other way to put it."[5]

Transgender people are not the only group of people targeted by far-right organizations like Turning Point. Another example closer to home for Turning Point is its own erasure of gay supporters of Turning Point itself. Kirk and Turning Point used to support gay conservatives, but some in the evangelical world saw this as evidence that Turning Point was not religiously conservative. A 2018 editorial in the student newspaper of the conservative Hillsdale College argued that Turning Point "is nothing more than a misguided attempt to make a difference and true conservatives should have seen that from the get-go."[6]

Turning Point used to have a gay conservative as a prominent contributor. But Rob Smith, a veteran who came out as gay in 2018, quietly left Turning Point after Kirk's turn to Christian nationalism. In fact, the Turning Point page dedicated to news about the "LGBT community" was last updated by an article by Smith in 2021. Before the turn to Christian nationalism, Kirk was unwilling to have Turning Point take sides on the political issue of gay marriage. This was likely a practice based on his claim made before the turn that groups like the Moral Majority in the '80s tried wrongly to force their positions on the nation. Kirk defended Smith from antigay slurs at Turning Point events in 2018. By 2023, Smith was facing those same slurs unprotected at a pro-Trump event.[7] And in 2024, Kirk affirmed "God's perfect law when it comes to sexual matters" by noting a verse in Leviticus that says those who commit homosexual acts should be stoned to death. "Just saying," he added to his radio audience.[8]

Reinventing the Old Way

In the seven mountains movement's plan for the mountain of family, the masculine heart is called into action as a kind of national moral guard for America. Men have long been primed for this call due to the use of military tropes amid a supposed crisis of manhood in evangelical churches. The mandate movement also aims to convince women to fashion themselves as spiritually minded homemakers. The feminine mystique—Betty Friedan's term for the societal expectations that limited women to roles inside the home—must be upheld and women trained to return to their most valuable roles as wife and mother. They are the guardians of the home so their husbands can protect the nation. In short, the movement wants to build up for national and community leadership a minority of White evangelicals through family building. To conquer the mountain of family, they need husbands who will become key leaders on the other mountains. Those people will defend and empower the traditional nuclear family in massively impactful ways.

To strengthen the family means to attack those who supposedly weaken the institution of marriage by embodying alternatives to the one-man-one-woman partnership. For decades, leaders of conservative Christian movements wanted homosexuality banned and sought to frame the gay "lifestyle" and "agenda" as evil, a threat to the family. In the '70s, state and local leaders tried to ban homosexuals from teaching in public schools. Exodus International spread the idea that homosexuals could be converted to heterosexuality. (Decades later Exodus rejected so-called conversion therapy and eventually closed.) In the '80s, an antigay pamphlet claimed that homosexual habits posed "a much greater threat to public health than smoking." The writer of that pamphlet, Paul Cameron, was expelled from the American Psychological Association in 1983 after misrepresenting research on how "gays are disproportionately responsible for child molestation and other violent crimes," and yet his work is still cited today by evangelical Christians.[9]

Kirk speaks about transgender identity in the same manner that previous generations of the seven mountains mandate spoke about homosexuality. To a church audience in 2023, Kirk said that identifying as transgender is "a throbbing middle finger to God."[10] In a social media post on International Women's Day in 2024, Kirk noted that Americans were mostly "accepting and polite" and that they "used to let crossdressers (as we more accurately called them back then) do their thing without harassment. What we didn't do was pass rules and laws 'normalizing' and 'celebrating' clearly pathological behavior, then making kids participate and invading women's spaces. Let's go back to the old way."

The "old way" for Kirk apparently ended during the Obama administration. In speaking about gay marriage to an evangelical audience in Arizona in 2024, Kirk said over the last decade or so that evangelicals laid down their "arms" and gave in to a "fake peace treaty" in that battle of the culture war. He added that evangelicals should have never "allowed" gay marriage to happen. That kind of claim—that Christians tolerated those who broke the moral code and so incurred God's wrath as a church—has long been part of the seven mountains mandate movement. A particularly powerful example dates back to the '80s, when HIV—initially called a punishment for gay men—began spreading beyond the gay population. Evangelical leaders of the time then concluded that AIDS is the fault of Christians because they "did not adequately fight the societal acceptance of homosexuality." The "logical conclusion" to this claim is that gays infected with AIDS should not merely be quarantined but that there should be "massive action to stop non-monogamous, non-heterosexual activity in its entirety."[11]

Two Books for Two Genders

Along with homosexuality, Turning Point has reanimated fears about one of the oldest cultural boogeymen for American evangelicals: feminism. While it didn't start the feminist "waves" of activism and advocacy, Betty Friedan's 1963 expose on American womanhood, *The Feminine Mystique*, continues to loom large in the evangelical ether. A leader in the evangelical feminism movement recalled fifty years after its appearance that the book was an eye-opener for "married, white, heterosexual women" but that "the churches, for the most part, were not dealing with this, except to condemn it."[12] Eventually theologically conservative churches did more than condemn the book and the larger subject of feminism. They asserted their own solutions to the "problem with no name" that Friedan described—except to those churches the problem wasn't what Friedman described. The problem as laid out in tomes on the role of wives and mothers was a lack of submission to husbands and God. That submissive role would be where women could become the people God intended and live a fulfilling life, opposite the angst in Friedan.

On that same fiftieth anniversary of Friedan's work, a female writer for the evangelical network the Gospel Coalition wrote about the impact the book had on her life: "I imagine I wouldn't have received my Master of Divinity at a conservative evangelical seminary, nor other countless opportunities I take for granted, had it not been for the questions Friedan's book raised." But the writer notes that the "identity crisis persists in women today as it did back then," and it is "unfortunate many believed Friedan's solution." The writer seems to count herself among those unfortunate believers, as she writes that she was led during the writing of her article on the book to "repent before the Lord for holding onto memories that would be fuel for resentment and bitterness toward men."[13] This sounds similar to a popular female TPUSA speaker who told Kirk in 2023 that "modern feminism was destroying women's happiness."

Feminism also had a detrimental effect on men, according to American evangelicalism. In the decades after Friedan, if evangelical women were confessing bitterness toward men (and their husbands specifically), churches began confessing they were not reaching men as they should. In the '90s, a crisis in evangelical manhood arose. Groups such as Promise Keepers sought to bring men back not only to church but to their biblical role as husbands and fathers. Founded in 1990, and in many ways peaking in the broader American culture in 1997 with a rally in Washington, D.C., Promise Keepers was the embodiment of its founder, former Colorado Buffaloes football coach Bill McCartney. Four years removed from a national championship, McCartney resigned his coaching position, putting all his attention on the ministry. It is not surprising that as Promise Keepers returned to its stadium rally roots in 2024, it put Kirk on its speaker lineup.

As historian Kristen Kobes Du Mez argues in her 2021 bestseller *Jesus and John Wayne*, the answer by Promise Keepers to the existential question of manhood is that men should be "tender warriors." Stu Weber's 1993 book by that name, *Tender Warrior: God's Intention for a Man*, sold 700,000 copies. While the former Green Beret turned pastor advocated for male protection of women and the role as a warrior in God's army, it also defined a man as having "a tender heart beating beneath his armor."[14] Turning Point has referenced this book in its commentary on masculinity.

But this isn't the only book that seems to have influenced Turning Point. By the turn of the twenty-first century, the response to the crisis of manhood in evangelical culture had reached such a crescendo that the opening of one of the best-known books on evangelical manhood frames its pitch as freeing men from all previous attempts: "I know. I almost want to apologize. *Dear Lord—do we really need another book for men?*" This comes from the introduction to the 2001 book *Wild at Heart* by evangelical author John Eldredge, which became a phenomenon in White evangelical churches as much as Friedan's book was in her own era of American culture. It was a book that set out the premise that adventure, wildness, and freedom were in the heart of men: "The masculine heart needs a place where nothing is prefabricated, modular, nonfat, zip lock, franchised, on-line, microwaveable." And we can only find this kind of place outdoors, "where the geography around us corresponds to the geography of our hearts." Eldredge contrasts this wild manhood with what he claimed had become of it in the '90s: "something more sensitive, safe, manageable, and well, feminine." To Eldredge, the '90s were an era of massive "gender confusion," when men were told to act like women, especially with regard to "minding [their] manners." But he adds that the "damage to masculinity" began in the '70s. To undo that damage, Eldredge said he was offering ancient invitations to men: a battle to fight, an adventure to live, and a beauty to rescue.[15]

These two books present key moments in the ascent of the family mountain by groups associated with the mandate movement. Eldredge especially was the foundation for a network of ministries to men that presented a picture of American evangelical men as fighters, warriors, and mountain climbers, both metaphorical and literal. Many, though, found the William Wallace–esque call burdensome and confusing.

Years later, Turning Point has returned to that well. But Kirk and Turning Point are not merely repeating decades of "pro-family" rhetoric. There is a distinct change in tone, a new and militarized aggressiveness that combines machismo with a definite and defiant political agenda embodied in the man White evangelicals put in the White House in 2017. This aggressiveness aims not merely to revive the masculine heart so that its body will protect wives, mothers, and daughters from the growing list of gender-deviant villains, but also to shame the rest of us for not being manly enough.

Manhood for the Nation

What defines the new aggressiveness of Kirk and Turning Point on the mountain of family is the translation of a personal quest as proposed by Eldredge into a national political fight. Turning Point has remade the central individual theme of Eldredge into a political, communal claim against totalitarianism. This change can be seen most clearly when one views the original cover of *Wild at Heart*, which featured a lone figure, pack strapped to his back, hiking under a setting sun, the image in a pink and orange hue. In Turning Point's hands, Eldredge's outdoorsy personal quest has morphed into a pseudo-military-style training event for a future war akin to the one fought by American colonists for independence from Britain.

Turning Point developed a series of events called "The Summit" and in 2023 offered four of these events that took men through physical exercises and Bible studies in mountainous locales to prepare them "to serve their God, their family, and their nation." These events aimed "to revive the masculine heart . . . by creating men who are physically, mentally, and spiritually fit." Not coincidentally, "reviving the heart" is a phrase often used by Eldredge. A thirty-second advertisement for the event shows shirtless men screaming as a voiceover says that spiritual "chains were broken" and "demonic influences" were sent away. Men are seen doing push-ups in a circle, carrying logs as a unit, and swimming together through muddy water.[16]

Another video about the event makes clear that modern liberal attacks on masculinity are the impetus for the event. As the video opens showing men arriving for the event, multiple male voiceovers read headlines about the rise of toxic masculinity. One voiceover quotes 2019 American Psychological Association guidelines meant to aid psychologists working with men: "Traditional masculinity—marked by stoicism, competitiveness, dominance and aggression—is, on the whole, harmful."[17]

The video then quickly cuts to a hip-hop song that begins with a record scratch and the words "Wait, hold up." Then men are seen working together to push large tires up hills and participating in a "trust walk," where one man leads a second, blindfolded man on a path. At the end of the video, the men create a cross from wood and seemingly all carve their names in it before praying as a group.

Kirk said the initiative was a pilot sponsored by a donor. The Turning Point website described a gathering in Montana involving twenty men, ages sixteen to mid-fifties, who learned how to be "strong men" and "servant leaders" through physical discomfort and training in "emotional intelligence." A daily schedule proposed early morning hikes followed by classes on "self-care," among other topics. The site said the participants became "real men."[18] Summit leader Spencer Mozingo, a retired Marine, led participants in hiking forty miles over three days. Mozingo described this physical work as part of the "breaking down" process that strips men of their "defense systems." Mozingo defined masculinity as a "balance" of strength and sensitivity. He added that "toxic masculinity" was a lack of control of emotion and aggression. He referenced Eldredge's book and its themes on "nature" and "finding purpose" as an influence.

Other groups targeting the same audiences use these same themes. One example is the Men's Alliance, a national network of weekly "rugged, outdoor workouts, and real-world devotions around a fire." It was started by a former Air Force pilot who believes "healthy men create healthy families, and healthy families create a healthy country."[19] But Turning Point turned that training into something more radical. On Kirk's radio show, Mozingo said that participants returned to their communities empowered and were now "standing up for what's right." He said at the end of the episode that "in order for the country to be saved, the church needs to be saved. In order for the church to be saved, men need to stand out and start being men." Kirk took that opportunity to apply the training to national politics by adding that strong men and the kind of masculinity taught by Turning Point at The Summit was the route to stopping tyranny in America. "When you don't have people standing in your way, it's easy to do whatever you want," he said, repeating Mozingo. "That is the roadmap for authoritarianism."[20]

Courage to Be Feminine

As Turning Point aims to create real men in response to the rise of feminism (and apparently tyranny) through these outdoor events, it is also teaching women how to be real women through their own events. Turning Point's Young Women's Leadership Summit is framed as an event that "uplifts women in a way to take back our country, our families, and our culture" by "restoring femininity and freedom over feminism."[21] The annual conference includes talks by social media influencers and Turning Point female staff. One 2023 speaker encouraged attendees to return to "biblical roots" of what women were "designed for." *The Washington Post* described the event as "embracing a particular kind of American nostalgia, one where women's liberation means being free from the complexities of modern gender politics."[22]

In her 2023 speech to the women's summit, Chaya Raichik, the owner of the provocative social media account Libs of TikTok (a partner of Turning Point)—whose followers often harass people, schools, and business leaders after the account puts them on blast for gender-related sins—framed the current American moment as a war on conservative attempts at cultural influence. Before listing some accomplishments—teachers fired, curriculum banned, books removed—Raichik complained about the liberal media "plastering my name everywhere," while her account gained millions of followers. She called coverage of her efforts "propaganda" and persecution. In 2024 Raichik used her self-described lack of training in politics and policy to get a seat on a board in Oklahoma that oversees libraries.

Raichik mused that she missed "the good old days": "Maybe I am old fashioned but when I was growing up there were two genders." Raichik promoted the courage to be conservative. She wanted the audience to ignore those who call conservatives names because being silent is the road to tyranny. She claimed her work on TikTok was a voice for "millions of Americans" who are angry as she is about the current state of America. And she spoke of "powerful forces" working against her.[23]

This echoed Erika Kirk (Charlie's wife), who entered the stage in a pink pantsuit under the output of confetti cannons. In her twenty-minute speech, she used evangelical language about spiritual battles and "the enemy" who could "take a foothold" in the lives of women, advocated for her brand of organic clothing, and praised Charlie as a father. She told women that they were "God's warriors" on the "front lines" of the nation's changing culture.[24]

In another setting, she specifically responded to Friedan's "problem that has no name," addressing women's fears about the lack of fulfillment as primary caretakers in the home. In a January 2024 podcast episode for a show dedicated to the "blessings" of motherhood, Mrs. Kirk tried to dispel that myth. "I think a lot of women think, 'OK when I get married or when I have kids, I'm stuck in the house.' That is not at all what it is." She said she wants women to create a home where husbands and children can find "rest and refuge" from "the craziness of the world that we are in today." She said the effect of such "guarding" of the home is to create husbands and children who are "fearless" when they enter the world and face whatever it throws at them.[25]

Erika Kirk's thoughts echo Bill Bright's advice to his spouse (who abandoned her career for their marriage) and the working order of married female staffers at his organization, Campus Crusade. Bright, of course, was one of the two men whose 1975 mountaintop experience became the origin story for the seven mountains mandate. According to a biography of Bright, married women on staff (who often were married to the male campus directors) made "domestic responsibilities their priority." A Campus Crusade brochure said that "the wife's first responsibility is to her husband." Early in the ministry of Campus Crusade in the '50s, Vonette, Bill's wife, struggled with the "frequent and elegant" entertaining she was asked to do by Bill and his expanding national travel schedule. Seeing this and other laborious homemaking duties as "monotonous," Vonette fell into what she described as "boredom and frustration . . . not unlike that described in Betty Friedan's book."[26] Later, in his 1986 book about the "nine spiritual war zones," Bright called the institution of the family "the key life support" for the nation. The soaring national divorce rate was part of an "invasion of worldly thought" into the evangelical church, he claimed.[27]

Loren Cunningham, the other man at that mountaintop experience with Bright, had a different approach to women. Cunningham, in fact, contradicted in practice more conservative theologians throughout the decades. Well into his ministry, he put those differences in print. In 2000 Cunningham wrote a book that offered a "fresh look" at the Bible on women and gender that sought to answer the "issue of women in missions, ministry, and leadership" that was "dividing homes, churches, communities, even societies."[28] From the beginning, Cunningham's Youth with a Mission permitted women to teach and lead, with his wife Darlene Cunningham a popular speaker in the ministry. Its teaching materials also offered a direct political and social reason to include more women as leaders and trainers of leaders: "When women are not given authority or are not recognized as equals to men through respect for their opinions, then authoritarianism is sure to follow."[29]

A Model for Marriage

If there was a debate about gender roles in the early years of the seven mountains mandate movement, Turning Point has chosen to stand with Bright and not Cunningham. In her message to the women's summit in 2023, Erika Kirk said it is important to have an "Ephesians 5 marriage." That is a reference to Ephesians 5:23: "For the husband is the head of the wife as Christ is the head of the church." She added a second Scripture reference to define womanhood in her speech to the 2022 summit. She told that audience, "It's OK to be a woman," albeit a "Proverbs 31 woman." To Erika, that meant it was good for women to be business owners and to pursue a career, as she had done. And when "the season comes to transition, it's OK to be a mother."[30]

Erika's use of Ephesians 5 and Proverbs 31 to define marriage shows the model she and Charlie want centered. Proverbs 31 describes a wife who buys and sells goods and fields. She is honored and praised by her husband for this work outside the home. But some conservatives have noted that the way in which many of their churches and ministries apply the chapter to women "weighs them down with unrealistic expectations and makes them feel 'less than.'"[31] Some liberal critics say, in fact, that the text "breaks with the submissive biblical womanhood model" because it shows women not only working outside the home but involved in activities that don't merely include husbands and children.[32] Read that way, Erika's career success and the continued growth of her business after marriage seems contradictory to her reference to Ephesians. But by centering these two parts of the Bible, Erika is implying that any work she does outside of the home is at least approved by her husband.

The Ephesians reference is used widely by those who support the marriage model of complementarianism. That model is grounded in chapter 5 verses 21 through 33, where those supporters see that the words of the apostle Paul create an authority or "head" within marriage (the husband as leader) and the wife in glad submission to help him succeed. Bright supported this view. He said a "biblical view" of marriage understands the husband to be "the shepherd of his family," while the wife "joyfully submits to her husband's authority.[33] Mary Kassian, a Southern Baptist professor writing for the conservative theological network the Gospel Coalition in 2012, noted that the rise of complementarianism came as both a word to describe the "equal, but different" roles for women and men and as a response to an opposite view called "role-interchangeability (egalitarianism)—a concept first forwarded and popularized in evangelical circles in the 1970s and 1980s by 'biblical feminists.'"[34] The divide between the two groups is best seen in their versions of submission in a marriage. One side sees female submission, and the other sees mutual submission.

While "complementarianism" became the label for the conservative position, Kassian noted early supporters chose it because other options like "traditional" and "patriarchal" were already associated negatively in the broader culture. It's certainly possible to conclude that Erika and Charlie don't use the term "complementarian" because of its own negative associations since its rise. But it is ironic that Turning Point now uses the word "traditional" and the trendy term "trad wives." In March 2024, to promote the next Young Women's Leadership Summit, the TPUSA Students Instagram account posted a picture of what it labeled the "Trad Conservative Starter Pack." Its caption made clear that TPUSA was implicitly lifting up "trad wives" as a good goal: "The girls that get it, get it. Join a TPUSA chapter today." The post includes images of a set of bridesmaids entering a small white church for a wedding, and a wife in a dress and apron feeding a taste of dinner to her husband in a '50s setting.

The Kirks as Model

Turning Point's plan for the family is epitomized by Charlie and Erika. What we know of their marriage shows itself to be refined through decades of conservative Christian theology. Each person brings a unique persona to the marriage: Charlie is the well-known face of Turning Point, national radio host, and political mover and shaker. Erika embodies the nurturing heart of the family. On the air, he is brash, provocative, angry, conspiratorial, and seemingly enjoys the daily political battle. On Erika's podcast, *Midweek Rise Up*, a listener will find episodes on love, patience, and mercy. While Charlie is the face of Turning Point marketing that includes merchandise with slogans such as "Don't comply" and "Ew, socialism," Erika's Proclaim streetwear brand sells clothes for babies and adults with Bible verses. The two personas are not completely confined to their separate spheres, however. Erika's site sells a sticker with the seven mountains slogan "Occupy until I come." And Turning Point sells a "Stay at Home Mom University" sticker to promote females not going to college.

Erika was a basketball player for two years at a small Christian college before transferring to Arizona State to receive a bachelor's degree in political science. As of 2024, she was pursuing a doctorate in biblical studies from the evangelical Liberty University. Charlie was a high school basketball player, though he never has said he had any scholarship offers and famously didn't go to college, though he wanted to. It is curious to see a person who has built the identity of his multimillion-dollar empire on the "scam" of college while married to a woman pursuing a doctorate. But it should be noted that Charlie praises a handful of higher education institutions, and Liberty is one.

Both have enthusiasm for politics. In a September 2020 episode of her podcast, Erika encouraged women who are passionate on social media about cultural topics to vote. She said that ignorance was not bliss when it came to politics. She argued that just as God established the family, he also established the civil government, the "source" and "foundation" of which is God. "Why would you retreat from that sphere of influence in life?" she asked her listeners, repeating the commonly used metaphor of Christians as "salt and light" in the world. Erika frames her religion as nationally powerful. She said in that episode Christians "preserve our country and even the world for that matter from decay." She then shared verses about "positioning Christian leaders" in political offices. While the version of the Bible she reads from uses the pronoun "he" seemingly to apply to all people who would be chosen for leadership, she doesn't specifically offer the possibility that women should be one of those chosen (though she doesn't eliminate that either).[35]

Both Kirks see themselves as empowering other members of their gender. Erika empowers her female followers to see the public battle of politics as not boring, as she once thought it was, but as a way to honor God in their personal, daily lives. This is why Erika asked her audience at the 2023 Turning Point women's summit to vote for leaders who "protect and defend our Christian values." She also suggested through another verse that Christians who vote for "the wicked" will be judged by God.

Those wicked unnamed by Erika are named by Charlie. For example, in March 2022, during a stop on a tour by Turning Point Faith at Fervent Church in Colorado Springs, Colorado, Kirk challenged "every man across America" to "intervene" at swim meets where transgender people were competing in girls' events. "You need to show up to the sporting event and be like, 'This is not happening actually. You're not competing against my daughter.'" Kirk said that in a "1950s America" men would have done this: "The fathers of every other competitor would've come out of the stands and formed a line . . . saying, hey tough guy, you want to get in a pool? 'Cause you're going to have to come through us."[36] This call to protect daughters is part of a larger move by conservatives to demonize trans people and enforce a binary understanding of gender, while also promoting men as aggressive protectors of women.

The moments when Erika and Charlie have shared the microphone reveal even more how the Kirks see their marriage as a model for others. In one episode of Charlie's show called "Tough Love" from September 2023, Erika and Charlie answered questions posed by followers of Erika's Instagram account. Questions like, "How do you know if you found the one?" prompted both to say they just knew. Erika joked about a "grilling" she took from Charlie on a date early in the relationship. "And you passed the test," he said.[37]

To be fair, Charlie and Erika do not explicitly pose their marriage as a model. But they offer standards and advice as if it is. For example, on the September 2023 show, Charlie said husbands should not be cooking. "That is the wife's job," he said, with Erika agreeing. He was asked how women can "get a godly man." His response was, "Don't act like a feminist." Charlie also said that "real men" don't have female friends; if a man does, he is likely gay. He also said women—single or married—shouldn't have male friends. He also criticized "missionary dating," in which a Christian dates a non-Christian with the hope of a conversion. He also disapproved of interfaith marriages. Erika said that older single women (i.e., those in their mid-thirties) have become "hardened" by their lack of marriage. Charlie interjected and called them "bitter." Erika agreed.

On the subject of complementarianism (though it was not named), Erika responded to a question from a woman who was concerned about how she, as an "alpha female" at work—a leader, go-getter, even controller—could be different at home. Erika said that for the "alpha female," the husband "is always your alpha." Charlie also said that "deep down," women want to be led by men. "I totally agree," Erika replied and thanked Charlie for "leading our family so well."

Kirk and His Mentors

The call to male leadership in complementarianism is passed down from one generation to the next. This usually happens in the context of a mentoring relationship. After Kirk's turn to Christian nationalism and his more explicit approval of conspiracy theories, pro-White racism, and support of Trump, one might wonder if there had been any older man to mentor him in a different, more positive direction, would things be different? It's the wrong question. He had mentors, and they led him into this turn. Kirk has described over the years close relationships with two pastors in his life: Rob McCoy, a megachurch pastor in California who convinced Kirk to turn to Christian nationalism and, before that, disgraced megachurch pastor James MacDonald, who was pushed out from his Chicago church empire for abusive leadership. Each left their imprint. It is no surprise that Kirk has grown increasingly angry, divisive, and abusive in politics. It was not politics that did that. MacDonald modeled that vitriolic bombast before Kirk ever knew Trump.

In some ways, Kirk takes after one of the early leaders of the movement within White evangelicalism who sought to reclaim manhood in the 2000s: Mark Driscoll. He was the founding pastor of what became a large megachurch in Seattle called Mars Hill. Driscoll ultimately left Seattle under a mountain of abuse claims that left massive amounts of religious wreckage. He was and remains a brash, provocative preacher whose theology often uses ridicule—especially of men—to teach gender roles like those lived by the Kirks. After Mars Hill imploded in 2014, Driscoll moved to Arizona. Kirk had Driscoll on his radio show in August 2023, and Driscoll pitched his new book about the culture war. Kirk called Driscoll one of the best Bible teachers in the world. They shared jokes about "woke" culture and "beta males." Not once did Kirk mention Seattle or Driscoll's past.

Christianity Today did a long-form podcast in 2021 on the impact of the fall of Mars Hill. Mike Cosper, the host for the podcast series, framed the story of Mars Hill with the poignant question of why the (mainly White) evangelical church keeps "elevating leaders whose charisma outpaces their character."[38] The same question asked about Driscoll should be asked about Kirk. One might ask, why didn't Kirk learn from the fall of Mars Hill? Or even the danger of MacDonald? Or, as many people have noted, Donald Trump? The answer is that he didn't want to. He wanted their version of manhood to succeed. What did Kirk learn from them? How to erase history.

Driscoll once had a massive following. Kirk has more now. And now Kirk, like Driscoll, is seen as a leader to other men. In fact, there are many White evangelical men who look up to him for various reasons. And the pastors who sit with him on stage praise him as well. Would Kirk listen to someone now who told him the truth?

Danger to Democracy

Kirk is empowered because he is an heir to a decades-long plan to conquer the mountain of family. That plan has allied at times with more benign claims about the effectiveness of complementarianism beyond the home. A longtime defender of this model of marriage and its larger impact, North Carolina pastor and theologian Kevin DeYoung, argues that the absence of patriarchy brings "dysfunction and desperation": "What school or church or city center or rural hamlet is better off when fathers no longer rule? Where communities of women and children can no longer depend upon men to protect and provide, the result is not freedom and independence." For him, anarchy will reign if patriarchy is not established.[39]

DeYoung doesn't dismiss democracy, only "enlightened" democracy, a nod to nations run by both genders. Defending democracy has not been part of the larger project of complementarianism. For example, the well-cited tome *Recovering Biblical Manhood and Womanhood*, published more than a generation ago, doesn't reference democracy in its pages. Turning Point has turned that absence into an antidemocratic pulse. For example, while Erika Kirk promotes voting, she notes wives can ignore current affairs at least for a "season," that season being young motherhood. But Erika doesn't cross the line to saying women shouldn't vote. In a September 2020 episode of her podcast, Erika referenced a woman who wanted her husband's vote to stand in for her own. Erika's reply was that anti-Christian policies could be passed under that logic; righteous candidates needed every vote. While Erika pushed back against that specific example, the idea has support among females who are platformed by Turning Point. Lauren Chen, a Turning Point contributor, has questioned the Nineteenth Amendment, which guarantees women's suffrage, and the democratic ideal of "one person, one vote."

If there is one analogy for advocates of the seven mountains movement for how the nation should be ordered, it is their definition of family. How the family should be ruled is how the nation should be ruled. Government and community led only by men is not a leap based on the movement's own words. This is why the mandate movement is a danger to democracy. It seeks to silence, erase, and eliminate voices.

Chapter Five

Marketplace Apostles in God's Economy

The Mountain of Business

In October 1979, Pat Robertson, the founder of the Christian Broadcasting Network and the face of its flagship talk show *The 700 Club*, wrote "A Christian Plan of Action for the 80s."

Coming from such an established figure in the American church known for healings and other charismatic efforts, Robertson's call for revival was not surprising. But what was surprising was that Robertson's list of the top five issues facing the nation during the second half of the Carter administration did not include the moral morass on the lips of many preachers in the era.

The preacher instead turned into an economics professor. Using the anniversary of the Great Depression as a launching pad, Robertson argued against Carter's policies on inflation, currency, productivity, and government regulations. Liberal ideas about the relationship between government and the economy since the '30s had been successful in a different time, he conceded, but now they were constricting growth and helping the Communist enemy gain ground on America. This should mean less spending, particularly on social welfare programs conservatives thought bred helplessness. These policy ideas had emerged as conservative Christians reengaged government, particularly in response to the federal government's threat to remove tax exemptions from churches that ran afoul of the 1964 Civil Rights Act.

Robertson then turned back to his sermon skills to paint a dark picture of the future of America. In response to the coming demise of the United States and the West, Robertson wanted Christians to get involved in government, media, and education. Robertson also made a plea to his fellow Christians to "learn the ways of finance." They should "learn and apply the principles of God's kingdom dealing with the acquisition and use of wealth." In other words, once made rich by divine aid in the marketplace, business leaders "should recognize the enormous good they can accomplish with that wealth." Interestingly, just a few years later, in 1984, Robertson had a warning for his fellow Christians who would find success in finance: people with too much money often have "too much power and will use it to oppress others."[1]

Making His Mark on God's Economy

Like his forefathers in the seven mountains movement, Charlie Kirk has repeated Robertson's pitch to wealthy Christians. In 2023 Kirk asked a collection of them to help Donald Trump get back into the White House. That group was organized by a Silicon Valley entrepreneur named Ken Eldred, who for decades has funded the seven mountains movement. In his pitch to the group, Kirk framed the needed money as part of a spiritual war. Naming wealthy liberals such as philanthropist George Soros, whom Kirk and allies have framed in recycled anti-Semitic tropes, Kirk asked the donors, "Why are secular people giving more generously than Christians? . . . It would be a tragedy if people who hate life, hate our country, hate beauty and hate God wanted it more than us."[2]

Where the next pile of money comes from is how Kirk is making his mark on the seven mountains plan for a Christian America. For Kirk, conquering the mountain of business means fulfilling the prophecy spread by the mandate movement called the great transfer of wealth. This is when God takes wealth from the evil rich and gives it to his remnant of true followers, who will use their new financial power for God's agenda. In Kirk's view that means deposing socialism as the demon atop the mountain of business. Referencing Soros to the donor group is part of a larger targeting of the

Hungarian philanthropist by many on the right. Soros, through his Open Society Foundations, has promoted education, transparent government, and progressive causes, yet many on the American right have wrongly linked him to supporting socialism. To Kirk, those who "hate America" like Soros want to keep socialism atop the mountain of business for one reason made clear during his pitch to the donors in 2023: They are not merely secular. They are anti-Christian. Kirk says God wants capitalism as America's economic system. While some prophets of the great transfer of wealth have said it can happen supernaturally, many others have said it would happen through the marketplace, where Christian entrepreneurs win against evil competition through innovation. And these individual economic victories will help God take dominion back from Satan in the nations.

Kirk's capitalistic rhetoric is not new. Previous generations of conservatives like Robertson have warned against anticapitalist ideologies dating back to the National Association of Evangelicals in 1943 and the sermons of Norman Vincent Peale blasting unions in the '30s. To them, keeping America economically free from such a threat was a straightforward, if not simple, plan of government inaction to keep markets unburdened from regulations on business owners big and small, including taxes. For Kirk, too, the government is the enemy. But Kirk's plan is an implicit rebuke of Robertson's caution about power and money. For Kirk, the link between power and money makes the former attractive. With money comes the power to keep the government from that money. This is why he says he is a supporter of cryptocurrency. It's "a decentralized way that everyday patriots can build wealth, store wealth, transfer wealth without big daddy government monitoring, infiltrating, observing, or preventing your God-given right to own private property."[3] In the last few years other prophets of the great transfer of wealth have also promoted the currency.

To amass more power, Kirk wants money and lots of it created by Christians who then can oversee a nation built on God's economy. Kirk calls Christians to this vision through his interpretation of words used by a prophet in ancient Israel: "Seek the peace and prosperity of the city to which I have carried you into exile. Pray to the LORD for it, because if it prospers, you too will prosper" (Jeremiah 29:7).

As previously mentioned, Kirk often uses a more forceful verb than "seek." But it is also important to note that to press his economic mandate, Kirk changes another word when he cites this verse. He changes "city" to "nation," something no English Bible translation does. While others in the seven mountains movement have dreamed of creating Christian cities, Kirk and Turning Point have often decried cities as crime-filled and soulless. He changes the reach of the verse to emphasize the national political movement that has become Turning Point. But also by changing the word to "nation," Kirk is nodding toward a desire of prosperity for a certain land, a home base of a certain people. Nationalism is never far from Kirk.

And Kirk's version of Christian nationalism has its own economic growth theology. To become a wealth creator, Kirk said at a 2023 conference for training attendees to think like millionaires, people should turn to the parable of the talents from Matthew 25:14–30, interpreting it as a call for more "multiplication" in the economy.[4] The parable's multiplication framing has long been used by the seven mountains movement.

Kirk is not merely a pitchman to the Christian millionaire class. He is now a member of that class. In the last few years he has created enormous wealth, much of it hidden from view. Kirk's riches known to the public include the six-bedroom, six-bath 6,800-square-foot home in a suburban Phoenix gated community he bought in 2023 for more than $4 million. Less than a year later, he sold it for almost $6.5 million.[5] He also bought a condo in Sarasota, Florida, in 2019 for nearly $600,000. While his salary from Turning Point is public and in range of other high-budget nonprofits (about $400,000 based on 2023 disclosures), his income from media contracts—from Salem Radio, book publishers, paid speeches, and TV appearances—is not known. Kirk also is not the only one who has garnered wealth through Turning Point's many arms. In 2023 the Associated Press reported that Turning Point has "enriched Kirk and his allies," who "steered at least $15.2 million to companies that they, their friends and associates are affiliated with."[6] Turning Point has created wealth or has offered opportunities to others to create wealth by allowing smaller start-ups to sponsor Turning Point events. Those can cost companies up to $250,000.

With that has come pointed criticism. Some have called what Kirk does a grift. In 2019 Charlie Sykes, former editor in chief of the conservative website The Bulwark and author of *How the Right Lost Its Mind*, said, "If I had to make a scale of the worst grifters on the right, Turning Point USA would be top of the list."[7] Grifting is done by a con man, a person who doesn't believe the lies he creates. Kirk is no stranger to lies and using lies to raise money. But from all accounts, Kirk believes in the seven mountains mandate and capitalism as the divine method for wealth creation. This is why Kirk also often paints a fear-filled future of a nation without the ability to create wealth. He has said in the past that capitalism empowers groups such as Turning Point and other national institutions of ingenuity that better our society. These groups could "wither under socialism."[8]

But that doesn't address how the money is made. Whether or not Kirk is greedy, how he made Turning Point into the indispensable organization for the seven mountains movement is simple. He expanded to new markets. Yet Kirk's wealth creation has come at a cost to the nation. As the fulfillment of the great transfer of wealth prophecy—that which claims to take from the evil and give to the good—Turning Point's power comes from money, money that has already, in Robertson's words, started to oppress others.

Prosperity and Prophets

The theology behind the seven mountains movement's call for wealth creation is the prosperity gospel. Made prominent by televangelists like Kenneth Copeland, Oral Roberts, and later Benny Hinn and Creflo Dollar, who taught different versions of the claim that God will financially bless his believers, the prosperity gospel gained popularity in the middle of the twentieth century "when the hope of postwar capitalism was embraced with religious fervor."[9] It took off because, among other reasons, the prosperity gospel's promised individual wealth works in tandem with free market capitalism.

Within that framework was born the vision of the transfer of wealth. Some, like Gloria Copeland, wife of Kenneth, date the prophecy back to a 1978 claim by an Arkansas farmer-turned-minister named Charles Capps, who saw a coming "financial inversion" of the world's economy in which God will empty the monetary "reservoirs of wicked men for days on end."[10] Capps once trained missionaries for Loren Cunningham's Youth with a Mission. He also had roots in the "word of faith" charismatic movement that taught people they would receive financial and health blessings if they only believed. He said that as he began to study the Bible from that perspective, "the first thing that changed wasn't my finances. It wasn't my crops. It was what I saw in my mind's eye. I saw myself rich. I was still broke, but I *felt* rich."[11]

There is some indication that the phrase "great transfer" or sometimes "great transference" of wealth comes from a concept from the early '80s called a "great outpouring of wealth." The chairman of Amway, long known as a procapitalism advocacy organization, in 1981 wrote that this "great outpouring" came from the "free markets" and "makes possible freedom from want, the creation of great works of art, of great hospitals, of great cathedrals, of great centers of learning, of so many aspects of the truly exceptional life." Those markets would be imperiled by government-enforced "income redistribution."[12]

In the late '80s, one ministerial advocate of the prophecy said an "outpouring" of "financial abundance" would allow Christians to rule the nations: "The gold in Fort Knox could belong to the Christians. The stocks on the stock exchange could be primarily bought and sold, and literally controlled by Christians. The oil wealth once dominated by OPEC, the diamond wealth of Africa, the plutonium wealth of Russia, the technical wealth of Japan, all of these and more, could be at the disposal of and in the possession of Christians who would carefully dedicate it to finance the Kingdom of God!"[13]

In the '90s, the Pentecostal global evangelist Morris Cerullo wrote about three wealth transfers in biblical history and how a fourth was slowly but surely happening. That didn't materialize. In his 1991 book *The New World Order*, Pat Robertson described a plan to take "the wealth of Europe and America and give it to" poor, third-world nations.[14] At the same time another prophet of the wealth transfer envisioned a "top-down" and "bottom-up" transfer. The former would happen when a righteous ruler's riches become available to Christian leaders. Joseph and the pharaoh of Egypt was a model.

King Cyrus of Persia—to whom Trump has been compared by advocates of the seven mountains—is also referenced sometimes because of his wealth and how he restored Jewish treasure after freeing Jews from Babylonian captivity. The "bottom-up" transfer would happen when a handful of economically successful Christians help others leave poverty, akin to spiritual venture capitalists who help multiply wealth in the Christian community.[15]

This seems to be the method preferred by the seven mountains movement. In the '90s and into the twenty-first century, this message about the power of Christian wealth was persuasive to a growing set of Christian businessmen. In this era of "marketplace ministers," the apostolic network led by C. Peter Wagner, the Fuller Seminary "church growth" professor, stood out because it offered something different from other organizations going after the same audience: a new title, "marketplace apostle." Like the religious authority, the marketplace apostle would command change for God within their industry and beyond through wealth creation. In Wagner's vision, these business leaders would function as "biblical entrepreneurs," who would also transfer wealth and reach the nation.[16]

This extension of traditional church-based apostolic authority was not an entirely selfless goal. It was an enticement to leaders in a sphere where the money was, godly money needed for the conquest of the other mountains. Wagner once wrote that the mandate movement will not see success without "large sums of money."[17] Wagner and his allies were not going to get very far financially with the institutional Christian church because they claimed denominations were under demonic control. It just happened that their new leadership network was independent of denominations. The apostles set out to convince business leaders their funds were not being used effectively for God's glory by their local church. And those who heard this pitch were more than eager to put down hundreds if not thousands for apostolic training. That money would become the early seeds of faith in fulfilling the great transfer of wealth.

The seven mountains movement initially hoped this accumulation of wealth would fund institutions to enhance the "total Christian lifestyle," such as Christian banks, Christian hotels, and Christian shopping centers, all to "keep the church at the center of the believer's daily life." One early model was "Baptist City" in Indiana.[18] The man deemed the father of the apostolic movement and who convinced Wagner to see new prophets in the world, Bill Hamon, envisioned these cities well into the '80s. These plans mirror the twenty-first-century plans for "thick Christian communities," as described in chapter 2. As Hamon wrote about his plans in 1981, both seemingly want to be "self-sufficient and independent of government control" and as exemplars "cause hundreds of millions to turn to Christ."[19] And the prophets would empower the businessmen to create the wealth needed. Hamon's 1987 book *Prophets and Personal Prophecy*—which turned Wagner to the growing prophetic culture—included a chapter for Christian businessmen who need "supernatural assistance" from prophets for business success because Satan has set his army against such success.

Hamon the salesman and Hamon the prophet were one and the same. Like so many, at first he was giving personal prophecies, giving divine permission to pursue a certain career path or encouragement amid failure. This is what happened to Hamon; in 1953 a prophet came to his church and confirmed his desire to enter ministry. As his ministry grew, Hamon's prophecies grew beyond the individual. When he first met Hamon in 1996, Wagner said Hamon broke the "spirit of poverty" within him by having Hamon and his friends stuff his pockets with cash. Wagner spent the money that evening on an expensive dinner with his wife that included a bottle of wine.[20]

Door to Dominion

While building a divine city from the ground up eventually floundered, a contemporary of Hamon's, Dennis Peacocke, began in the '80s to suggest that Christians not engaging with the culture—and therefore not "occupying" until the master returns (per Luke's version of the parable of the talents, Luke 19:13)—had allowed American cities to be infected "with political and social programs totally at odds with the laws of God's universe."[21] As he wrote in 2003, this gave a mandate to Christians to touch "the gears and levers of the economic mechanisms that drive the entire world."[22] That many versions of Scripture translate Luke 19:13 as "Do business until I come" has been well used within the seven mountains movement.

In this context, Lance Wallnau had his fortuitous meeting in 2000 with Loren Cunningham about the seven "mind molders" and then envisioned the seven mountains. Wallnau's whiteboard became ubiquitous across the world in business training seminars as the visual of the seven peaks he consistently drew on it. Wallnau's new metaphor gave entrepreneurship in a free market a divine energy. Influence became conquering. Success became transformation. Stewardship as a kind of passive caretaking of resources became actively taking back money once used for evil.

One could say Wallnau was the right person at the right time—a visionary given a marketing scheme from God just when it would work best. But Wallnau is not the only or the central reason for the spread of the seven mountains. What seems most obvious now more than two decades after Wallnau met Cunningham is that the spread of the mountain metaphor was due to the networks Wagner organized, the ministries founded and pushed forward on the gifting of one person and the donors linked to them. That was the initial marketplace for the mandate and its list of areas. It had been primed for decades by the prophecy of the great transfer of wealth. Wallnau's individual charisma and skill certainly helped, but the mountain of business was a ripe opportunity long before he came along.

In that light, it is not a coincidence that Wallnau first described his vision for the seven mountains in several 2005 essays about "transformational coaching" of business leaders. Like other concepts in the seven mountains movement, this was not unique to the movement. The phrase dates to the '90s in executive training. The editor of the book that includes Wallnau's essays, who was from the Pat Robertson–founded Regent University, had stumbled onto the topic during a sabbatical and transformed the secular idea into a plan for Christian leaders in the marketplace. Wallnau's essays argued that only "a transformed leader" could be "trusted" to rule the earth. And these "transformed" leaders have bigger goals than changing churches. They "will not stop until they have a transformed nation." That would come as business leaders gained and transferred wealth: "Your giving works like a bulldozer to plow up satanic obstacles."

He claimed that the more these "breakthroughs accelerate," then "something more than a revival can take place," something like a "tipping point in the national culture." In his words, a "reformation in the last days" when nations will be judged.[23]

Victims and Victors

In her history of the prosperity gospel, Kate Bowler notes that it "guaranteed a special form of Christian power" to disappear societal ills such as racism and poverty.[24] For the seven mountains movement, the special power is the power of the free market. One of the obstacles to the transfer of wealth was a demonic spirit of poverty, the spirit that Wagner said he was released from by Hamon. The spirit of poverty kept the poor from seeing divine economic opportunity. To arouse them to create their own economic success in the free market, they were called by the movement from "narratives of victimization and into narratives of self-determination."[25] As one church in New York City put it, "Jesus loved the poor but never endorsed a spirit of poverty." That church argues that leaving this spirit behind "involves renewing our minds to align with God's perspective on wealth and abundance."[26]

While Wagner got a pocket full of cash, the movement's plan to eliminate the spirit of poverty includes a combination of discipleship and discipline toward wealth creation. More than thirty years ago, a missionary with Loren Cunningham's global evangelism group Youth with a Mission wrote that the poor "should be encouraged to participate in the liberation from their own poverty" and given opportunities to create "the wealth to meet their needs."[27] At the same time, Black megachurch preachers like T. D. Jakes began to call out a "victim mentality that precludes many African Americans from reaching their potential."[28]

While at times Charlie Kirk has decried "identity politics" or segregating politics by race, Turning Point continues to deliver the message of free markets to markets outside its predominantly White audience. It has specifically promoted the antivictim message to racial minorities. In 2022, the Black man known as the MAGA Hulk, Stephen Davis, wrote for the Turning Point website that a "victim mentality has gripped this generation, this country really." Without mentioning a specific race, Davis said that racism "isn't holding these people back—it's their own mentality."[29] In 2022, another Black ally of Turning Point, Rob Smith, wrote directly to Black men, telling them that even though they are told they are victims of their surroundings, they should "take control" of their life: "You have been blessed with the power to create your life, so it is your responsibility to do so."[30] Turning Point began in 2019 to create merchandise with the victim and victor message that tried to convince minorities to downplay systemic obstacles to their economic and personal success.

Turning Point's original messenger to African Americans was the Black social media influencer Candace Owens. She was hired by Kirk immediately after he heard her speak at a conference hosted by long-time conservative activist David Horowitz in November 2017. Kirk told *The Washington Post* in 2019 that "the media says people like her don't exist."[31] By "people like her," he meant Black conservatives, especially ones as aggressive as Owens. During her two years as director of urban engagement and then communications director for Turning Point (2017–2019), Owens echoed Kirk at every turn about Black prosperity and the power of the free market. From the start, she embraced the role of combatant in a cultural war using the same framing about victim and victors.

Owens has said that Black Lives Matter protesters had embraced a victim mentality and that the Black community had disintegrated because so many Blacks had been "brainwashed" to believe "there is value in being a victim." She spoke of her grandfather as someone who lived the American dream even though he started out as a sharecropper. He eventually bought the farm that he had worked. Owens defined the American dream this way: "You can start anywhere in your life and end up somewhere else as long as you are willing to not play the victim."[32]

Owens eventually started a campaign to persuade Blacks to leave the Democratic Party. At its height in 2020, the campaign, known as Blexit, took in $7 million in donations.[33] The effort stalled amid a cratering of donations beginning the next year and is now a small part of the massive Turning Point empire. In 2023 it took in just under

$275,000. The campaign repeats some of the same rhetoric that Kirk and Owens have used. It acknowledges the large generational wealth gap between Whites and Blacks and even admits that the source of the gap is racism, but it is adamant that the wealth gap persists "because the black community is not taking advantage of financial growth opportunities," like life insurance and saving money.[34]

While Owens was paraded by Turning Point as someone who could claim victory over her circumstances, her origin story is filled with moments of her as a victim of systemic racism and poverty, collective national sins that groups such as Turning Point ignore. She grew up in poverty in Stamford, Connecticut. She was the target of a racist attack by fellow students at her Connecticut high school in 2007. She went to college but left in her third year from the University of Rhode Island without a degree and with $150,000 in debt.[35] After working in New York, she was part of a failed attempt to start a business in 2016 that would have publicly named "cyberbullies and trolls." To many, especially early victims of such people who were critics of the business, this meant doxing or publishing broadly not just their names but their locations. In-person harassment usually has followed doxing. In response to her business idea, people began to dox Owens. She blamed progressives (though with "scant evidence") for this. After getting supportive contacts from conservatives, Owens said she "became a conservative overnight."[36]

It's hard to speculate on the religious training Owens may have received while being reared by her grandparents after her parents divorced. Did she attend a prosperity gospel church as a child in Connecticut? Who knows? But with her own words, Owens is practicing a form of the prosperity gospel. It is her "victim to victor" narrative that bolsters her status in the marketplace, to paraphrase a study of female prosperity gospel preachers.[37] Each failure is a test of faith—not so much in God, though there is that. Rather, it's a test of faith in the gospel of prosperity, a test of faith in her own entrepreneurial spirit. At a 2022 event Owens said, "I believe that God picks people to have experiences in their life. The good ones and the bad ones. I believe that God wanted me to have my parents. I believe that my God wanted me to grow up in a house that was dysfunctional. I think that he wanted me to grow up impoverished. He wanted me to go through a hate crime. . . . Who better positioned to attack the left's narrative than somebody who has lived through all of that?"[38]

Turning Point and Kirk have held up Owens as a successful example of how individual innovation in the marketplace from those who grew up in poverty or amid racism can create wealth. But while Owens gained economic success, she didn't innovate. Instead, she resurrected long-debunked conspiracy theories, especially about Jews. She became a victim of her own making. This revival began at a 2018 Turning Point event in England when Owens downplayed the Nazi regime and said it was only Hitler's "globalism" that made him unacceptable.[39] (Calling Hitler a globalist is both inaccurate and ironic, since the term is often used as an anti-Semitic slur.) The backlash to Owens's comments was massive. Turning Point chapters—never known for public dissent—publicly asked for Owens to go.[40] By May, Owens had left Turning Point. In the ensuing years she continued embracing anti-Semitic rhetoric, leaving the Daily Wire in 2024 with a pointed rebuke by the conservative media group's founder, Ben Shapiro, who is Jewish.[41]

Owens has become a pariah among conservatives even among those who first supported her. In 2023 the David Horowitz Freedom Center—the group that sponsored the panel where she met Kirk in 2017—said her words, especially about Jews, had become "morally obtuse."[42] In 2024 Dennis Prager, the Jewish conservative who hired Owens after she left Turning Point, clearly suggested she is an anti-Semite.[43] While Owens remains a fixture at Turning Point, it created a website to distinguish her opinions about Israel from Kirk's.

Old Racism, New Markets

The story of Owens is not merely an example of the seven mountains movement's plan to address poverty. It is also part of Kirk's shift toward the seven mountains, a move that has dramatically changed both the movement and his organization. The end of the Owens era at Turning Point preceded by just a few months the era of Kirk's turn squarely into Christian nationalism and the seven mountains mandate. But also the end of the Owens era began Kirk's descent into pro-White rhetoric. These two are related.

One might immediately wonder why, if Owens left Turning Point under pressure for pro-Hitler rhetoric, did Kirk almost immediately become pro-White himself and turn his growing politically powerful organization to the same? In other words, why did Kirk decide to exploit America's racial divide at the same time the Black woman he handpicked to spread the message of capitalism became too toxic for him? The answer is capitalism. Turning Point's audience and its market of donors and supporters clearly didn't want the anti-Jewish message. But there was a market for anti-immigrant and racial-division messages. One can believe Kirk simply became convinced of the seven mountains mandate. And one may also rightly believe he changed the course of Turning Point in 2019 to embrace those new racially motivated markets because that is where the money was.

Why Turning Point needed new markets is a complex question. In 2019 Kirk and the organization were aging. And doing the same campus tours every year isn't exactly the best example of innovation, but then in the spring of 2020 came the pandemic, which kept Kirk from doing those tours. By then California megachurch pastor Rob McCoy had convinced Kirk he could enter a new market, the one market he had criticized as wrong-headed not a year earlier: largely White evangelical churches embracing political partisanship like they had in the '80s. Kirk began touring them in lieu of college campuses during the early years of the pandemic.

At the same time Kirk was being trained in the seven mountains mandate, he was apologizing for his "loose" immigration policy after White nationalist critics claimed he and Turning Point were not anti-immigrant enough.[44] (Kirk had said America should offer green cards to international college students when they graduate.) While one can reasonably assume that Turning Point donors played a role in Owens leaving the organization, Kirk said people he respects also pushed him to make that immigration statement. That apology was a first step toward a second new market for Turning Point. By 2022 Kirk was posting about "an undeniable War on White People in The West."[45] He attacked George Floyd, "wokeness," Black pilots, and Martin Luther King Jr. He expanded from those into broadsides against "perceived instances of 'anti-white' bias," according to a 2024 profile of Kirk in *Mother Jones*, which made the case persuasively that Kirk now embraces "racist and white nationalist rhetoric and figures with little hesitation."[46] Beyond Kirk's comments, he also hired a former producer of Fox News's *Tucker Carlson Show* who resigned after he secretly posted racist and sexist remarks in an online forum. Kirk has also spread the "great replacement" conspiracy theory that claims the American "left" wants to replace "America's white population" with immigrants.[47] Doing all this made Kirk the leader of the "next generation of aggrieved white conservatives."[48]

Critics stood in line to claim overt racism. After Kirk's criticism of King, a Black pastor who has long supported Trump told NBC News, "I've got to say, racism is like the word 'ugly.' I can't always describe it, but I know it when I see it. That boy's a racist right there."[49] Kirk and Turning Point have always vigorously denied that he or the organization have any link with White supremacy or any other racist ideology. He has specifically denounced neo-Nazis who have shown up at Turning Point events. He has consistently said no one should be judged by the amount of melanin in their skin. And Turning Point has shunned the handful of its followers on campus whose racist texts or comments were exposed. And yet the change to this market is clear.

The impact is also clear. While the anti-Semitic toxicity of Owens forced Turning Point to part ways with her, Kirk's pro-White rhetoric has brought in millions both to Turning Point and himself. Not coincidentally, at the same time Kirk became a sycophant of Trump, who made his start in politics with a 2015 campaign kickoff that specifically targeted Hispanic migrants and from there has linked himself to White nationalist groups and racial violence. Trump as a market of one also has had a profound impact on Turning Point's financial status. Trump has appeared at many Turning Point events, his Florida resort Mar-a-Lago has hosted a Turning Point fundraiser, and Kirk's rise in conservative politics can largely be attributed to his sustained defense of Trump. Like the other new markets, appealing to Trump as a market furthers the claim Kirk turned Turning Point to political and cultural divisiveness for the wealth transfer.

Democracy and Capitalism

These new markets have changed Turning Point. And because the organization with Kirk as its face is a kingmaker in conservative politics after the reelection of Trump in 2024, they are changing the nation in a negative manner. The demon atop the mountain of business may be socialism for Kirk, but socialism is not the most pressing threat to the nation's economic health. That threat is what Kirk has become: part of a new elite, a "godly" one, which now has economic dominion over America. He leads a religious oligarchy akin to the initial vision of marketplace apostles by forefathers of the seven mountains movement. Their wealth empowers them to reshape the culture to their desires. In a world where the wealth of Christian nationalism is aimed at every sphere of influence, each success of the movement comes with a significant cost to democracy, and its success on the mountain of business may be the most impactful. Democracies die when the elite use their money-made power to oppress others. It's clear that Kirk and Turning Point continue purposely to refuse Robertson's warning.

Chapter Six

What's Really Happening

The Mountain of Media

The screen fills with dramatic music punctuated by horns and softened by string instruments. A slowly spinning globe appears, the outline of the Florida panhandle seen from space, lush and green against the blue water surrounding it. Then amid sweeping yellow banners, the announcer bellows the words that have begun this newscast since its first episode in 1980: "From the heartland of America to every nation on earth, this is *Jack Van Impe Presents*—the truth in news and commentary."[1]

Tonight's episode is from August 2013. The televangelist Jack Van Impe—at this point in his early eighties, his silver hair still full and his pink tie contrasting with his dark suit—sits at his usual spot, to the right of his wife, Rexella, who anchors the broadcast from their studio in Michigan. The show begins with her soft but serious voice: "We are going to be talking once again about some things that are very relevant to all of our lives." There is trouble in the Middle East, missiles aimed by Iran at Israel. There might be war. But not just any war, a "worldwide war."

Later in the show, looking directly at the camera, Rexella says, "Friends, I can't imagine it. Can you? A horrible war that will be worldwide. If we've got a worldwide government and we've got somebody over it all, we're going to have a worldwide war. Thank you, Lord, that the book of Daniel has been open and we know really what's going on, how to react. So I'm going to ask Jack, will this world war really happen?"

As promised in the show's introduction, the truth in news and commentary will come as Jack Van Impe—the man known as a walking Bible for his memorization of the King James Version—will reveal how prophecies of the Bible are being fulfilled before our very eyes. His quick citation of verse after verse from the prophecy written by Daniel (and other apocalyptic scriptures) crescendo into his prediction that the signs point to the imminent return of Jesus. One of the signs is the appearance of a new world order, the final global government in the history of humanity. That order is the resurrection of the Roman Empire. "It's the last sign and it's here," Jack Van Impe says, almost breathlessly, during the thirty-minute show.

God and the News

Before Lance Wallnau's mountains, a significant segment of American evangelicalism was devoted to an end-times theology known as dispensationalism, named for the ways it divides eras of history into dispensations. Using a literal interpretation of the Bible, John Nelson Darby developed dispensationalism in the nineteenth century, and it reached the masses through the publication of Cyrus I. Scofield's *Scofield Reference Bible*, which was the first Bible in English to add commentary alongside verses. This meant that readers could "search out connections between Bible verses with similar themes through 'cross-references.'" That kind of work allowed them to unlock the "secrets" of Scripture, and the searching for secrets "became an intricate quest as passages from one book of the Bible were sought to provide clues for understanding other passages."[2] Published in 1909, the Scofield Bible garnered lots of attention in evangelicalism during the decades of global conflict in the twentieth century because of how it presented the darkness of the last days: wars and rumors of war, the abomination of desolation, but most especially that rebuilt Roman Empire, chosen because of the metaphorical power of the seven hills of Rome, spoken about in the revelation given to the apostle John, who was exiled to Patmos in the latter part of the first century. As Jack Van Impe wrote in his commentary on that apocalyptic text,

"It locates, geographically, the final world power block and headquarters for the world church" in Rome. The "world church, sitting on those seven hills, heading up scores of denominations, rides to power" on the strength of that new world government.[3]

Van Impe often used seven as a mnemonic device. Besides the seven hills, there were seven global governments in history, seven signs of the end-times, and seven modern global organizations that pushed us toward the apocalypse. These included the "illuminati," the United Nations, and the "new age movement." Of course, there was also the key feature of dispensationalism: the seven-year tribulation during which the world, absent Christians long "raptured" away, would descend into chaos. This violent end to the world would bring with it an intense desire by those who taught the rapture to understand the signs of its coming. This understanding was also part of the gospel imperative. Dispensationalists and their eschatology (study of the last days) of premillennialism—the belief that Christ will return and rule for a literal thousand years—used the end-times as a motivator for evangelism. Judgment is coming, and you should be ready.

Why might this matter in a chapter on the mountain of media? Van Impe's claim to the truth in news and commentary was based on facts that to him couldn't be denied. In so doing, he and others like him during the rise of dispensationalism taught Christians to see through the headlines and understand the times, to use the Bible to interpret the news. They read the world's end through a journalistic presentation of contemporary events.

The seven mountains mandate movement is not a collective advocate for dispensationalism like Van Impe. But while including a spectrum of beliefs about the last days, the movement has copied Van Impe's approach to news. Secular media remains, in their view, the devil's well-financed and well-ensconced propaganda machine with no end in sight. So the plan to Christianize America and destroy democracy begins with developing a highly tuned conspiracy radar. Spiritual paranoia—to think all the time as if there is a conspiracy against God—is what drives the seven mountains mandate. And that paranoia is both the message and the medium of their media. Those who "know" what is really happening, those who "see" the big picture, conquer the mountain of media. It empowers people who won't be controlled or brainwashed by the mainstream media. A conspiracy mindset is what unites these people. But it is also what destroys democracy because it removes them from any broader community conversation. While this minority is always hopeful to convince others and create a majority, the burden of the truth is its own reward for this mountain.

This paranoia mindset is not unique to the movement nor even unique to religious people. The paranoia in American history was pointed out famously by historian Richard Hofstadter in his 1964 essay "The Paranoid Style in American Politics." He wrote that some politicians had secularized a "religiously derived view of the world" that reduced public issues to good and evil. This mindset is a sense that "all our ills can be traced back to a single center and hence can be eliminated by some kind of final act of victory over the evil source."[4] The seven mountains mandate, though, is not merely stoking paranoia in government or politics. It suggests there is a massive seven-headed conspiracy in America that has taken over all our cultural institutions.

Republicans overall have been prone to accepting conspiracy theories during the Trump era, but White evangelical Republicans in particular have become more receptive than non-evangelicals. One study found that 67 percent of White evangelical Republicans believed that "an unelected group of government officials, known as the 'Deep State,' were working against the interests of the Trump administration," compared to 52 percent of White non-evangelical Republicans.[5]

This is not surprising, given the theological legacy inherited from people like Van Impe and how it has been enflamed by seven mountains advocates in recent years. For example, at an event in February 2023 Charlie Kirk said, "There is no other way to explain the campaign of arson and destruction against our country other than diabolical spiritually dark influences that are fighting for dominion over this nation."[6] While Van Impe and Kirk might both agree that "God wins in the end," Kirk thinks God wins by establishing a Christian nation, not removing Christians through rapture as Van Impe thinks. In August 2022 Kirk wrote that the "left" was trying to maintain power through any means, but that this "final point in the war" for Western civilization will end victorious for Kirk's side.[7] For Kirk, when the war ends, Western civilization will be the ground for that Christian nation awaiting the return of Jesus.

To win that war, the seven mountains mandate movement does not merely expose conspiracies as Van Impe did; it calls Christians to act against them. For example, Johnny Enlow, one of the pastors turned prophets due to his investment in the seven mountains, called in his 2009 book for Christians to create "redemptive" news. He predicted the rise of a national newspaper that will have the "perfect balance of hope, truth, and reality checks."[8] These "checks" are those which expose conspiracy.

To convince its audience to act as Enlow envisions, the mandate movement suggests Christian inactivity and ignorance give power to the conspiracy. It turns the passivity created by waiting for the end-times and the imminent rapture into an urgency to stop the prophecies once made by obsessed media figures like Van Impe. By suggesting that God alone was moving pieces around a chess board to defeat Satan, the dispensational picture of a sovereign but hidden divine strategist made the audience for that worldview passive, waiting for whatever God had in store. The waiting, of course, made many impatient, and so many prophets started to name the date and time of Christ's return, tying their prophecy to scripture passages that foretold the very news they were seeing in the newspaper and on TV. Van Impe was not immune from that. The mandate movement saw that impatient energy and pointed it at a new target. During an appearance at a church in San Diego in 2023, Kirk lovingly mocked people who send him emails announcing Jesus is returning within the week and by effect no further political action is needed. His response to that "poor theological" position was this: "If you believe that Jesus is coming back soon you should have the opposite view. You should be leaning in. You should be taking terrain. You should be pouring in. You should be acting more courageously and boldly, not retreating."[9] "Taking terrain" is a commonly used phrase by advocates of the seven mountains mandate.

Mediating Conspiracy

Listen to any Christian nationalism advocate and at some point they will name the conspiracy at the heart of media. The mainstream mass media doesn't tell you the whole story, they say. Those media outlets have an agenda, and they don't know God. These attacks on the media go back decades. One might consider that longevity as a failure for the mandate movement. The war to take back the nation's airwaves, spurred by people like Jerry Falwell in the '80s, has long been lost. No one is trying to win control of a mainstream news network, as Falwell suggested he might do in 1981.[10]

Instead, American conservatives started a media war against mainstream news. Fox News, which first appeared in 1996, and radio influencers like Rush Limbaugh, who became nationally syndicated in 1988, were the first shots in that war. Since then, many Fox News anchors have spread conspiracies, pumped misleading segments, and publicly endorsed outright lies, such as those about the 2020 election. Limbaugh's audience has fragmented to other hosts, and his ratings juggernaut of a show has been replaced in many ways by the Salem News Network, the fifth-largest radio group in the nation with more than 2,700 affiliates. On the television side, Sinclair Broadcasting, which promotes conservative propaganda, owns or operates 185 stations in eighty-six markets as of 2024. Then there are outlets like One America News Network that are even more radical, populating an even more conspiratorial news feed filled with fear and division. Amid the mass media ecosphere fragmenting into niche audiences, conservative bubbles have hardened over the years into enclaves of lies and outrage.

American evangelicals also now have their own influencing operations. According to one scholar, by 2019 the "electronic" church of American evangelism included (1) ten national radio networks, each controlling up to 500 outlets, attracting six million weekly listeners, and one-fifth of the total radio stations in the nation, airing "religious teaching, talk, or music formats"; (2) at least a dozen television networks with a reach of 100 million households, with fifty syndicated programs with weekly audiences near seven million; and (3) content on demand that streams "across every digital media platform."[11]

This is what one of the first Christian media-made celebrities, the televangelist Pat Robertson, hoped to see when he wrote, "Christians must become aware of the awesome power of the media to mold our moral and political consensus."[12] There is a reason Loren Cunningham called the seven cultural influences "mind molders."

Francis Schaeffer took aim at one of those mind molders through his analysis of media. One chapter of his book *How Should We Then Live?* was dedicated to "manipulation" by the "new elites." Those elites were the major media institutions in America, from the *New York Times* to CBS. To Schaeffer, the demon atop the mountain of media is not secular media itself. Rather, it's an ideology that entrances Christians to accept the media as neutral: "humanism."

To show this, Schaeffer attended to the editing of the news, especially as it reports on events defined as news by these elites. Through editing, "an aura and illusion of objectivity and truth is built up, which could not be totally the case even if the people shooting the film were completely neutral."[13] Schaeffer made a film series based on *How Should We Then Live?*, and in the episode on media manipulation he created the scene of a small riot on a dark city street, with protesters and police pushing and shoving. His commentary to the audience noted that the same scene would be shown twice, with a different journalistic voice-over on each. One voice presented the event with a bias toward the protesters, while the other supported the police by calling them "guardians of the peace." Schaeffer's thesis was that "consciously or unconsciously" the media has "become an instrument for manipulation" because it as an institution is empowered by humanism. To Schaeffer, humanism is "man demanding to begin autonomously from himself and turning away completely from anything God might have to say." And authoritarianism may arise from the government, but the more pressing danger is that it will come from the "vacuum" filled by humanism and the loss of a Christian worldview in any nation.[14]

Humanism as a philosophy is centuries old. Humanism as a conspiracy against American Christianity is only decades old. Historian of American Christianity Martin Marty said in 1981 that American evangelicals created humanism as a conspiracy: "Whenever you wish to organize a group in America, as diverse and pluralistic as we are, you have to focus on a bogeyman."[15] The tactic was in use by the mid-1970s, when an Arizona congressman "introduced an amendment to withhold federal funds for any educational activity involving 'the religion of humanism.'"[16] By 1980 in a book about humanism dedicated to Schaeffer, the conservative minister and later author of end-times novels Tim LaHaye warned that humanism had controlled America and if Christians didn't wake up, by the year 2000 it would control the world.[17] Humanism among other ideologies replaced the Antichrist as a single political leader that would rule the world in the last days. Moving from identifying not a person but a political ideology was a key early step in the creation of the seven mountains movement. More than forty-five years after LaHaye's claim, Kirk claimed in a 2022 speech that "our nation's young people are being targeted by The Enemy," who is attempting to "turn" them toward "secular humanism."[18]

The thesis that journalism, and the media more broadly, is a secularizing force in modern America is not new. What is secular about the media, according to this thesis, is not just that it is godless. It is also a secularizing force because, as a professionalized institution, it uses science, reason, and facts to speak authoritatively about the reality of the world, effectively replacing religious truth tellers with media voices.

This is why some in the mandate movement and beyond imagine the mass media as part of a larger anti-Christian conspiracy. There is, of course, fear of another religion embedded in this conspiracy. There is a long history within Christianity of linking media manipulation to Jewish puppet masters. To answer that media-based conspiracy, the anti-Christian conspiracy mindset created the need for truth tellers who know how to help others identify conspiracy. As Lance Wallnau posted on social media as recently as August 2024, "What we need are strong voices, grounded in truth, who can cut through the noise and help us stay anchored in God's word, ready to stand firm against the deceptions swirling around us." This returns the power of truth telling granted to journalism back to Christian leaders like Wallnau and Kirk. Not only will those leaders and their media empires teach you the Bible, but they will teach you the news too.

Conspiracy at the Start

Kirk has created a multimillion-dollar national brand based on unveiling the conspiracies at the heart of American media godlessness. In 2020, Salem Media started to air Kirk's daily three-hour talk show. According to data shared by Turning Point with NBC News in 2024, Kirk's podcast "is being downloaded between 500,000 and 750,000 times each day," ranking it in the top 15 on Apple Podcasts for news. Phil Boyce, the senior vice president of Salem Media Group, called Kirk a "force of nature" who "is also the most profitable host in our network with the most total affiliates and the second most radio affiliates."[19]

It should come as no surprise given how Kirk got started. His entrance into politics, you'll recall, was a 2012 Breitbart post written while he was a senior at Wheeling High School in suburban Chicago, claiming that the Advanced Placement economics textbook used in his school was indoctrinating students by not giving conservative economic thought equal space. Here was an unknown student speaking to millions of readers of the leading alt-right website, sharing insider info the mainstream media would never cover—what was really happening on the ground in education. What was happening was a conspiracy, according to Kirk: "This economics book is only a microcosm of the indoctrination children are receiving in today's public schools, as unionized teachers push a liberal-leaning agenda."[20]

Then there was Kirk's own origin story for why he got into politics in the first place. It also rests on conspiracy. In a 2015 speech he claimed he was denied admission to West Point and his spot was given to "a far less-qualified applicant in my district that was of a different gender and a different persuasion," implying—and later saying overtly—that he believed this other person "may have been admitted because of affirmative action."[21]

As Turning Point grew, its media coverage of the supposed conspiracy of indoctrination in high school grew to higher education and beyond. Kirk said that students can't even identify when indoctrination is taking place. Turning Point and its resources were the answer. It published a book in 2015 called *How to Debate Your Teacher (and Win!)*. It framed a massive educational conspiracy: "Today, teachers and professors all across the country are training young minds to believe that capitalism is immoral."[22] Kirk moved on to conspiracies in government, noting in a 2018 editorial that there was a "deep state" or an "entrenched, highly ideological, ethically unencumbered" shadow government of bureaucrats that was conspiring to stop capitalism.[23] By the summer of 2023, when Donald Trump was indicted in Fulton County, Georgia, Kirk claimed all the conspiracies were working together against Trump and his movement, saying in a tweet that "it's all orchestrated and harmonized." Kirk told his radio audience in a video linked to the tweet, "Let me tell you what is really going on here. Because this is deeper than just the indictment. This is a top-down exhaustion campaign. . . . This is psychological warfare." He added, "You have been participating whether you realize it or not."

The Production of Conspiracy

Not surprisingly, to help its audience realize their position amid vast conspiracies aligned against them, Turning Point employs known conspiracy theorists. One of Turning Point's nineteen "contributors" is Jack Posobiec, a former Navy intelligence officer. According to the Southern Poverty Law Center, Posobiec is the "most active spreader of disinformation" among the "anti-democracy hard right." He helped to amplify a conspiracy theory in 2016 about child sex abuse in the basement of a Washington, D.C., pizzeria or what became known as "Pizzagate."

To empower conspiracy, Turning Point uses an in-house investigation team called Frontlines (the same group that organized a sting operation at a Nebraska Walmart). Its reporters have been sent to the U.S.-Mexico border to ride along with law enforcement. That aided conservative influencers like Kirk who on the issue of immigration peddle the "great replacement theory," which claims there is a conspiracy to replace White people with non-White people by allowing undocumented immigrants to cross the southern border unchecked. Turning Point also produces what might loosely be called documentaries with on-the-ground reporting that aim to debunk conspiracies. One documentary is the fourteen-minute video about life in Cuba hosted by Benny Johnson called "Everything You've Ever Seen about Cuba Is a Lie." The title itself implies a vast conspiracy to hide the truth about the economic status of the Communist island.

The Turning Point media apparatus aims to give its audience "today's headlines" and "timeless truths." But any claim to truth by Turning Point is highly questionable. The website Media Bias/Fact Check as of 2022 ranked Turning Point's credibility as "low," saying it is a "questionable source" based on its spreading of "propaganda, conspiracy theories, and numerous failed fact checks." The group Ad Fontes Media labels both Turning Point's website overall and Kirk's radio show specifically as "unreliable" and "problematic." Politifact has checked claims by Kirk sixteen times, and only two could be labeled in any way as "true."[24]

The logistical production—the manpower, the time, the creation of content—of Turning Point's media in general is significant. But Turning Point also works to maintain audience interest in specific conspiracies by framing them as having anti-Christian goals. Turning Point's pushing of the "Great Reset" is a good example. Turning Point did not create that name; it is the name of an initiative pushed by the World Economic Forum in response to the global economic crisis after the initial rise of the COVID-19 pandemic. But Kirk and Turning Point's version of the Great Reset is a nefarious global agenda that threatens free markets, Christian worship, private property, and more. Kirk told the National Religious Broadcasters in 2022 that "what we need right now is a new Great Awakening to stop the 'Great Reset.'"[25] In a 2023 ad to sell his book about this conspiracy, Kirk told his audience that they should fight back against this "sinister" plan, but it wasn't just books and speeches by Kirk that drove Turning Point's conspiracy work for the better part of a year. The conspiracy played a starring role in a 2022 conference called "Futures," held at a megachurch run by Turning Point ally Jack Hibbs. At the conference Kirk framed the Great Reset as standing against the Christian assurance of victory. Its advocates, he said, "talk openly in their philosophy about what they think eternity will be. The merging of man and machine, for example, the uploading of consciousness. This is very important. . . . They are taking

Christian eschatological promises and then hijacking it for their own purposes."[26]

In fact, it's Kirk who has hijacked the Great Reset. He literally read from the stage of the conference a passage from a book written by the head of the World Economic Forum, Klaus Schwab, that highlights the opportunity to "reimagine" our world after the pandemic. He then tied such reimagining to the Bible, specifically the story of the tower of Babel in Genesis 11, where humans tried to build a tower to heaven and God destroyed it. Kirk and others see the tower construction as a story about a one-world government, or what many in the seven mountains movement call the "new world order." "This kind of spiritual battle is unfolding right in front of us as articulated in their playbook," Kirk added.

Bad biblical application is only part of the conspiracy-promotion strategy, though. Every conspiracy needs a vague set of characters, a group working against God. The World Economic Forum fits that bill. But the conspiracy also needs a vision, the godless manifesto set to change the world in a terrible way. Kirk claims that Israeli history professor Yuval Noah Harari, who has spoken at the World Economic Forum, is the source of the vision of "merging of man and machine." In his 2018 speech at Davos, Harari said that "in the coming generations, we will learn how to engineer bodies, and brains, and minds."[27] From that and similar statements, Kirk claimed in 2023 that Harari and a larger crowd of unnamed World Economic Forum supporters are "a group of self-declared gods in the 21st Century" and "they have all of man's accumulated knowledge and cutting-edge technology at their disposal."[28]

In fact, Harari is not advocating for this future but warning of its massive problems. Harari made that clear in an interview he gave in 2020. In a question-and-answer session with viewers, he said we have a "huge gap" between "our power and our wisdom," adding that we often misuse the former to "upgrade humans into gods." Furthermore, in his 2020 speech to Davos, Harari gave a "blistering warning" about all these issues.[29]

Why has Kirk gone to such lengths to frame an organization and one person as such a threat to humanity, when in fact this person echoes Kirk's own fears about global power? One answer is that Kirk knows the audience to whom he sells his conspiracies. No matter what end-times theology American evangelicals may follow, all of them have been taught for decades about a global dictator and the rise of one group that overtakes the world. Kirk is preying on that history. A second answer is that Kirk wants to frame himself and his organization as the truth tellers standing against any attempt to snatch the victory of God's kingdom from his followers. Sadly, the reality is quite different.

Maintaining a specific conspiracy, though, must end at some point. That is because pumping one specific conspiracy too long runs counter to the larger strategy. One must invent new examples to keep the focus on conspiracy. Much like the early prophets in the seven mountains movement who kept pronouncing again and again anti-Christian actions by larger, often-unnamed global forces, Kirk and Turning Point keep reinventing the wheel to keep the engine moving. This is why the massive action Turning Point conducted against the reset conspiracy eventually stopped. By 2024, there is little trace of the conspiracy in Kirk's expansive media empire. One can still find the digital ad Turning Point made to sell Kirk's book, a few articles on the "live" news feed archive Turning Point maintains, and a handful of videos buried on the Turning Point YouTube page, all created in 2022. Kirk's YouTube page has no sign at all of the Great Reset, however, and he hasn't been quoted in a news story about it since 2022.

The obvious question then is if this conspiracy was so terrible and so powerful, why have Turning Point and Kirk stopped talking about it? They have moved on from the very danger they told so many about because to maintain the threat of danger, new dangers must abound.

Conspiracy as Danger to Democracy

Conspiracy as a strategy will continue to have detrimental effects on American democracy. Kirk and Turning Point aim to disrupt the deliberative part of democracy by creating not merely an alternative set of facts, history, and culture, as the Christian media movement did in its origins, but also by eroding trust in democratic institutions.

In short, conspiracy as strategy leaves no way to unify around shared American ideals nor any way to deliberate about them in new and helpful ways. Mundane disagreements are always shadowed by larger conspiracies.

Conspiracies as strategy create factions that don't engage with others, only seeking to overcome the enemy through defeating the larger conspiracy. And to many, the traditional or "mainstream" media aids and abets that conspiracy. Melissa Sell, a Pennsylvania resident, told the Associated Press in 2024 that "if it's a big news story on the TV, the majority of the time it's to distract us from something else. Every time you turn around, there's another news story with another agenda distracting all of us."[30]

There are many people like Melissa long engulfed in one conspiracy after another. The sham of conspiracy is that it pretends to give its consumers a sense of engagement. What it really leads to is a never-ending loop of public division. Despite the danger of that, Kirk doubles down on the persona he has crafted: truth teller. In his appearance at a church in 2023, Kirk urged his audience to look at what they have failed to do as an answer to the question of what they should do in the future: "If you have not lost anything significant in the last couple of years, you're a spectator and you're not in the arena." He listed several things he has lost, including relationships with family members. The pastor on stage with him and the crowd applauded.[31] This kind of approval of sacrifice for conspiracy is a threat to democracy. It is what built the media silos Turning Point has taken advantage of. And it is the plan for Turning Point for the foreseeable future.

Chapter Seven

The Left Can't Meme

The Mountain of Entertainment

Two years before the mountaintop vision shared by Bill Bright and Loren Cunningham, the third person most often associated with the seven areas of cultural influence was well on his way to influencing culture. By 1973 Francis Schaeffer's trilogy on Christian apologetics had made him an evangelical celebrity.

That year he published a short treatise called *Art and the Bible* framing his principles for art and its relationship to Christianity. He summarized the wide presence of art from poetry to drama in the Christian scriptures and offered standards on how to judge art. Schaeffer urged Christians to create art out of a Christian worldview. Doing so would persuade non-Christians of that worldview, most especially the truth and beauty of God.[1]

Schaeffer's idea that Christian art should compete with secular, even anti-Christian art and offer the public a contrast in content has been the overarching message from American evangelical leaders ever since, many of whom have noted that he influenced their thinking. Consider the 2008 book *Culture Making* by Andy Crouch, former editor of the leading evangelical publication *Christianity Today*. His book and associated interviews at the time repeated Schaeffer's criticism of fundamentalism's stance against culture and noted why there was such a lack of Christian entertainment. He noted in a 2007 interview that "for a while" American evangelicals "thought the best thing we could do with culture is to just condemn it. Sort of stand outside it and resist it and be suspicious of it and try to avoid it." But that didn't change the bad movies playing in the theater. "The only way to change what is shown on those screens is to make a different kind of movie that can compete effectively with the ones that are currently showing. . . . It's only when you make something different that the culture of the movie theater or the movie industry will change." In Crouch's words, "Culture changes when people actually make more and better culture."[2]

At the same time Crouch was affirming the strategy behind decades worth of Christian culture—from Veggie Tales to Thomas Kinkade to the Left Behind books and movies—there was another, growing strategy from advocates of the seven mountains mandate movement. They were not interested in merely offering a Christian alternative to secular entertainment. The movement wanted its cultural content to do more for the nation's politics. It went "on offense," to use the words of Andrew Breitbart, founder of the alt-right website that bears his name. In 2009 he argued that the electoral cycles of every two or four years was too limited in strategy: "Why didn't we invest 20 years ago in a movie studio in Hollywood, why didn't we invest in creating television shows, why didn't we create institutions that would reflect and affirm that which is good about America?"[3]

Breitbart's call for a cultural offensive came at the Conservative Political Action Conference in 2010. He targeted the "elitists" in culture: "You're not on our team. You're not on the American team. You're on the progressive team. We tried to play nice with you, and nice is over." In 2011 his site laid out that doctrine, noting pop culture as a powerful cultural influence. "If the Right has any interest in reclaiming that ground," it should invest in cultural content that tells the conservative story, the site claimed.[4]

This more aggressive strategy has always been in the DNA of the seven mountains movement. In *Kingdoms at War*, Bill Bright wrote about what became known as the mountain of entertainment that producing and consuming edifying content was important but that Christians should recognize the enemy's power: "We are subconsciously being programmed with thoughts that elevate the secular humanist world view." In a bit more aggressive tone, Cunningham said that Christians must "recapture" every form of entertainment for Jesus.⁵

Turning Point's vision for the mountain of entertainment has elements of edifying engagement like Schaeffer. Yet it emphasizes the purpose of entertainment as something else, something purposefully divisive as Breitbart envisioned. Turning Point's entertainment strategy is akin to its strategy for the mountain of family: erase that which isn't agreeable to its ideology. This erasure happens through belittling political opponents (with a side effect of tribal enjoyment!) so they think twice about participating in democratic arenas through entertainment. Instead of laughing along with comedic mocking from "elite" entertainment like *Saturday Night Live* and *The Daily Show*, Turning Point offers to mock the mockers. While Turning Point takes on genres long seen as unfriendly to Christian conservatives, its strategy for the mountain of entertainment also performs the culture war in arenas not usually known for such—namely, sports and pop culture, arenas it and its allies once honored as apolitical—creating new battlefields on purpose. These two areas build on the other arena where Turning Point first found success, an arena born for the internet age: memes.

Andrew Breitbart was well known for his mantra that "politics is downstream from culture." Charlie Kirk learned this strategy from the place he got his start, Breitbart News and its tagline "More truth, more fight." The Breitbart doctrine is now the Turning Point doctrine. One doesn't have to wait to see the long-term impact of this divisive strategy. America is seeing the fruit already.

Reclaiming Sports for Christ

Historically, with a few noted exceptions, sports for evangelicals have not been linked with a political agenda. Yet now they have been claimed as political by Turning Point. This action has been framed as a reaction to "woke" athletes. That means Turning Point and its allies both applaud athletes they politically align with but also aim to silence those athletes who make political statements with which Turning Point disagrees, accusing them of violating the "purity" or neutrality of sports even as they platform athletes who speak as conservatives. Silencing those narratives means Turning Point's ideology has no competition.

In 2021 Turning Point created a show dedicated to the intersection of religion and sports that aimed to "boldly disrupt the sports media industry by changing the narrative" and reclaim the conversation about sports for conservatives.[6] *Breakaway* ran from September of that year to July 2022. The host, Jon Root, a former in-game host for the San Jose NHL franchise, said he started the show with Turning Point due to the "over-politicization of the sports industry and our society."[7] The show sought to return sports to the "unifying" role it once played in America and expose how "the left is ruining sports." "Once we throw them and their crazy ideologies out of our games, we'll finally be able to enjoy watching again," Root said in a promo for the show in 2021.[8] The show featured Root interviewing athletes and coaches who had made conservative "stands," such as Joe Kennedy, the football coach who took his game-prayer case to the Supreme Court, and NBA player Jonathan Isaac, who stood during the national anthem while his teammates knelt in response to the murder of George Floyd in 2020. Root also criticized athletes and coaches who spoke out for more gun control, such as NBA coach Steve Kerr. Root argued in one show that ESPN had a "double standard" for having a "no politics" policy but "always" seeming to "empower and protect their talent that leans Left."[9]

In December 2021, Kirk was Root's guest on the show. The theme of the episode was "why America should look like sports." To Kirk that meant America should reward those who succeed by hard work and good strategy, as in sports. The best teams develop methods that are "unique and entrepreneurial and disruptive," Kirk said. Both Root and Kirk also agreed that sports were supposed to be an "outlet" away from politics. Kirk said he doesn't watch professional sports anymore due to "woke" policies and players. Kirk applauded hockey for "staying patriotic," even though most NHL players are Canadian. "The Canadians are more enlightened" about the goodness of apolitical sports than America. Kirk's solution to "woke" sports was more authoritarian owners: "The owners have to start to take responsibility and leadership and stop kowtowing to a small group of woke activists when in reality our country wants sports back. We want them back in a non-woke way."[10]

Kirk's claim that sports should be an escape from politics is also an implicit claim that it also should be free from other disputes, especially theological ones. His strategy to silence those who want to disrupt Turning Point's narrative about theology became clear in how Root's employment ended. Root was let go from Turning Point in 2023, though his show stopped production well before that. Root didn't leave Turning Point due to any sports-related opinion, but for critical theological opinions he had of pastors who were partnering with Turning Point. One pastor was Mark Driscoll, whom Kirk was promoting on his platform around the same time that Root criticized him on social media. Root also revealed in 2024 that his theological disagreements with Georgia megachurch pastor and Trump supporter Jentzen Franklin cost him his Turning Point job. Root wrote on social media that he told his Turning Point bosses he would only interview Franklin at a Turning Point pastors conference if he could ask Franklin about his advocacy for the prosperity gospel, a highly debated subject within American evangelicalism. Root wrote, "They had someone else interview him. A week later, I was fired," adding a shrug emoji.

Pop Culture and Cultural Sickness

The other "neutral" cultural arena that Turning Point began to war with to conquer the mountain of entertainment was pop culture. That effort began when it hired a little-known local Kentucky radio host who had a growing social media influence. Claiming as her platform the "conservative voice in pop culture," Alex Clark started her Turning Point show *POPlitics* in 2019. The show was billed as "a weekly show for those who love pop culture—without the propaganda."[11] This kind of mythmaking repeats the decades-old claim that the "left" controls entertainment.

But that is not the only false claim in the tagline. Like Root's sports show, Clark's show was full of overtly conservative propaganda. The first episode of *POPlitics* in October 2019 railed against Beyoncé's "hollow" life advice.[12] Episode 3 hinted that a movie star may be a conservative. Other episodes of ten minutes each followed weekly in which Clark sat on a white chair in casual clothes, her voice akin to anchors from *Entertainment Tonight* amid synthesized music, ripping through the headlines of stupid celebrity behavior and at times offering moral critique. One critic described the show as using "cursory mentions of" celebrities to "introduce a predetermined set of right-wing talking points," basically shoehorning politics into culture.[13]

Clark's position on the seven mountains mandate is unknown. But she has promoted forms of Christian nationalism, specifically promoting "America's history as a Christian nation," as she did on her *POPlitics*-related podcast called *The Spillover*. In one episode, Clark repeated claims made by Kirk about cowardly churches not preaching politics due to fear of losing members.[14] Other episodes promoted the "Great Reset" conspiracy theory discussed in chapter 6.

Just as Root had his disagreements with Kirk and Turning Point and felt its response, Clark too faced the power of the organization, though in a much bigger way. For example, while Kirk and others have long attacked the pop music star Taylor Swift, Clark is a self-admitted Swiftie. She was often the target of anti-Swift backlash from people she would otherwise agree with on social issues. During a particularly vitriolic week in January 2024 after conservatives attacked Swift for her Super Bowl cameos to cheer on her boyfriend, Kansas City Chiefs tight end Travis Kelce, Clark said she had "never been so emotionally exhausted and just done, just done with the conservative movement over this week." She added, "Maybe if conservatives put the same fervor into hating the left we would get somewhere with the conservative movement."[15]

Clark was also the target of more substantial harassment beginning in 2019 when Turning Point and Kirk began to be targeted by a collection of White nationalists who thought the organization and its leader were not pro-White enough. Clark told Vice in 2022, "I disgust them, because I wear makeup and dress trendy, and wear crop tops."[16] Turning Point, specifically its chief content officer Benny Johnson, later hired people from that same group. Kirk and Turning Point also later began to repeat pro-White rhetoric from the group, including the group's use of the rap song title "White Boy Summer." White supremacist groups had been leveraging the title since 2021, mainly through racist memes, and using it as a recruiting tool in the United States and internationally. At Turning Point's June 2024 "People's Convention" (where Trump was the headliner), Jack Posobiec "walked out on stage with a 'White Boy Summer' flag, and promptly threw out hats bearing the same slogan."[17]

Perhaps not coincidentally, Clark turned from pop culture as a platform shortly thereafter. She announced in August 2024 that she was ending her *POPlitics* and *Spillover* series. She said the change had been in the works for more than a year, and a month later she launched a new show called *Cultural Apothecary* that aimed to "heal a sick culture—physically, emotionally/relationally, and spiritually." One of the promos for the new show claimed that "health is non-partisan." One can certainly question that claim coming from a person whose previous show was heavily partisan, but it also echoes Clark's original claim about her propaganda-less pop culture show. That Clark would make the claim twice shows that the culture war remains a silent weapon in Turning Point's strategy. But its use by Clark in advocating for a show dedicated to healing may reveal the most important truth: the culture war has affected her negatively.

That war has impacted differently the two genders Turning Point recognizes. In her message to her audience announcing the end of the shows, Clark said, "There is an expiration date on who can do this type of content." She added, "You can't grow with it. Eventually I think it becomes strange to be a certain age covering it for longevity especially as somebody who is single."[18] Clark's candid admission is both about age and gender. Turning Point seemingly draws females in with pop culture only to suggest at some point they are too old or need to get married. And her audience of young female conservatives was aging as she was, many adding children and family. Clark turned with her audience and a larger turn within Turning Point toward homemaking as the role for conservative women, a political statement no doubt, though not as aggressively stated as others. That pivot was on full display at Turning Point's leadership summit for women in 2024 (see chapter 4). Many speakers there echoed Clark's topics on her new show, which include "Get Radicalized on Honey," "The Return of Big Families," and "How Crunchy Moms Will Revolutionize America."[19]

The culture war has had a different effect on males. Retreat isn't the response from the males in Turning Point. Kirk, with two children, continues his weekly podcast roundtable called *ThoughtCrime*, which has produced some of his most disturbing comments, including how Taylor Swift is "bitter and angry" and "out of eggs," Black pilots whom he "hopes" are qualified, and his desire to force children to watch televised executions. Benny Johnson has also turned his platform toward family building while continuing to be as dedicated to the culture war as ever. He posts Bible verses and pictures of his growing family (he has four children as of 2025).

These different effects on the genders are intentional and reflect the ideology of the seven mountains mandate movement. The retreat by females and the overt aggression by males (often pointed at females not in their tribe) in the scope of the mountain of entertainment parallels the mountain of family, where the role of each gender is clear: females create a space apart in the home, and males lead outside the domestic arena through politics, business, and other areas of influence that change the nation.

Memefication of the Mandate

Sports and pop culture as content are outgrowths of Turning Point's original medium: memes. If we understand sports and pop culture as channels to spread conservative talking points in Instagram-able quips and to answer the call for more "fight" among conservatives, memes were the original channel for that simplistic style of spreading combative ideology.

Before memes became associated with the viral internet combination of stock picture and (usually) sarcastic words, it was a concept scholars and cultural writers used to understand how thoughts and ideas spread. The man credited with coining the term in 1976, Richard Dawkins, notes his version of it was just that—a variation on other usages from other people. Dawkins's contribution to the definition of *meme* was that its spread acted like the self-replication of a gene. Instead of DNA copying, the meme was a unit of cultural reproduction, like music, fashion, and catchphrases.

In 2018 one writer for the BBC argued that the first memes (by our modern, image-based definition) were comics from 1921 that were "variations on the same style—using two panels and captions to set-up an expectation and contrast it with reality."[20] Others have pointed to the spread of a cartoon of a man named Kilroy with a long nose hanging over a wall during World War II. This image moved from graffiti to film and television in the '70s.[21]

Most importantly, the spread of ideas was a replication Dawkins compared to that of DNA. Yet memes in the internet age act differently than the meme envisioned by Dawkins. This is why one scholar of digital culture argues that the Greek rhetorical concept of *enthymeme* "better captures the essence of internet memes." Such memes are not marked best by their imitation, but "by the capacity to propose or counter a discursive argument through visual and often also verbal interplay."[22] Enthymemes work well because they often leave the conclusion—the action step, for example—unstated and therefore implied. Viewers often make that unstated conclusion explicit through applying the meme to their own experiences and knowledge. In other words, the internet meme is great at undercutting already established and therefore more powerful narratives, and it also allows an audience to identify with the messenger and message through their own emotional or rhetorical agency. It makes them part of the "in crowd"—in on the joke but also tied to the political and social message in the meme. This piece of art is also entertaining, often at the expense of a political enemy.

There is certainly room for debate on whether internet memes are art or entertainment. But they have a message. The seven mountains mandate can be seen as a meme for its use of Christian scripture as stock verses revised for its agenda. This is what Christian nationalism scholar Matthew Taylor argued in his 2024 book about the religious ideology that energized the January 6 insurrection. He wrote that the seven mountains "prophetic meme" is "like internet memes in that they keep getting repurposed and utilized in different ways." This and other prophetic memes "become part of the assumed vocabulary and culture even though they might have very little grounding in the Bible or traditional Christian theology."[23]

Turning to Memes

Turning Point's use of memes may not be surprising, especially given that Kirk is a younger millennial who graduated high school in 2012. The power and efficiency of memes as a medium for replicating well-worn conservative ideas was long in Turning Point's DNA before it turned to the seven mountains mandate. In 2016 and 2017 it often hosted a campus event called an "affirmative action bake sale."[24] The organization would "set up a table of cookies and a sign with advertised prices of $1.50 for Asians, $1 for Caucasians, and 50 cents for black or Hispanic people." When asked the reason for the different prices, a Turning Point representative would reply, "Certain groups get different opportunities than others and Turning Point USA believes affirmative action doesn't give equal opportunity."[25] That specific campus event has been conducted by conservative campus groups going back to at least 2003.

Yet that replication is not merely a copy. Turning Point has changed tactics, if not targets, after public blowback. In more recent years, Turning Point has changed the event to a "GPA Bake Sale" in which students with lower grade-point averages get lower prices for cookies. This "demonstrates the unfairness of socialism, because those who work hard should be rewarded," according to a Turning Point 2021–2022 chapter handbook.[26]

Once empowered by Trump in his first term as president, Turning Point turned its meme capital to helping Trump. For example, in 2020 Turning Point undertook a "months-long effort" of "deceptive online tactics," to help Trump, *The Washington Post* reported. The effort was conducted by teenagers, some of them minors who were being "paid to pump out" the messages at the direction of Turning Point Action, an affiliate of Turning Point USA. Repeating or using similar language in a massive amount of social media posts—acting like what experts call a "troll farm"—the campaign eventually caught the eye of social media companies. Twitter, now known as X, and Facebook suspended at least 260 accounts involved in the activity for "platform manipulation and spam." Facebook later banned the marketing firm that Turning Point was working with.

This was not the first time Turning Point's well-shared social media content had caught the eyes of others interested in divisive rhetoric for its political goals. In 2016 *The Washington Post* noted that a Senate assessment found a "Kremlin-backed" group "amplified Turning Point's right-wing memes as part of Moscow's sweeping interference aimed at boosting Trump." The report pointed specifically to the use of Turning Point content as evidence of Russia's "deep knowledge of American culture, media, and influencers."²⁷ Also in 2024, according to an indictment by the U.S. Department of Justice, a media company run by Turning Point contributor Lauren Chen paid its content creators with money from Russia. "That content was allegedly aligned with Moscow's political interests in the states, with a pair of Russia Today (RT) employees accused of shelling out $10 million for favorable pieces of media from the group," *The Daily Beast* reported. Two Russians were charged with conspiracy to commit money laundering and conspiracy to violate the Foreign Agents Registration Act. Chen was fired from the Glenn Beck–founded Blaze Media, and her Turning Point profile was removed from the organization's site shortly after the indictment.²⁸

Benny on the Block

One of the content creators who was paid by Chen's media group was the aforementioned Benny Johnson, Turning Point's chief creative officer. He posted on social media that he was "disturbed by the allegations" in the indictment and that he and the other "influencers were victims in this alleged scheme." Johnson was hired in 2018 by Kirk to start Turning Point's production arms. The story of how the seven mountains mandate movement changed from aiming to influence to fighting a cultural apocalypse can't be told without the impact of Benny Johnson on Turning Point.

While there is no evidence Johnson himself either believes in or disputes the seven mountains mandate, like Alex Clark, he has spread Christian nationalism myths about the origins of the United States. He told his online audience in 2024 that America's government at its founding was "interwoven" with the "nature of God." "And if you are looking to destroy this place," he said, "you must separate us from God."²⁹

The thin, White Johnson often drapes himself in the American flag in his headshots. His profile picture for his media company, The

Benny Show, often shows a smirk on his face. And the half-rimmed glasses frame has stayed constant throughout his career. A *Washington Post* profile called him "a skittish Clark Kent."[30] Before coming to Turning Point, Johnson worked at more-mainstream outlets, like Buzzfeed, and more-conservative outlets, like the Tucker Carlson–backed Daily Caller. He started out writing opinion pieces at Breitbart, like Kirk.

Johnson joined Buzzfeed in 2012. There he was the "viral politics editor" who wrote content that often went viral but was revealed in 2014 to have been plagiarized. Nonetheless, that 2015 profile in *The Washington Post* said he was "one of the most trafficked news writers on one of the most trafficked Web sites in the world," referring to Buzzfeed. That same year he was hired at a rising conservative outlet called the *Independent Journal Review*. Two years later he was fired from that platform after a six-month stretch in which he was accused internally of plagiarism and promoting conspiracy theories.

But even amid those black marks, Johnson made a name for himself. His exploits included writing a story about the funny way Supreme Court "interns sprint down the steps to carry a big ruling to their media bosses" and "the secret Dunkin Donuts inside the Library of Congress." The *Post* also noted, "And no one can ride a meme like Benny Johnson."

But he also was not merely a cultural observer. According to the *Post*, "He assigned his team to parade a cardboard cutout of Hillary Clinton through a conservative conference to film the reaction of the rambunctious crowd." While it is not known if Johnson played a role, that same antic was repeated at the Turning Point party at the 2019 CPAC convention in Maryland—except this time the cardboard cutout was Democratic Rep. Alexandria Ocasio-Cortez, a long-time Turning Point target.[31] The person who hired Johnson at Buzzfeed, Ben Smith, noted in a 2024 book about his time as editor that he erred by bringing Johnson on board. "I thought Benny could be the David Brooks or George Will of the meme generation." After the plagiarism scandal, Smith remembered how Johnson had been "probing" for an audience, "following the traffic where it led him." But also he had a "thirst for attention" and a "willingness to say absolutely anything to go viral."[32] Johnson eventually started using the title "Godfather of conservative internet," though the origin of that is unclear. When the far right NewsMax announced in 2020 it would host *The Benny Report*, it said Johnson had "earned" the nickname.[33]

Meme Warfare

By the time Turning Point hired Johnson it was already being referred to as a "conservative student-focused meme factory."[34] Turning Point's first viral meme was a variation on the decades-old conservative policy to cut the federal budget. "Big government sucks" as a message started in 2014, according to Kirk's 2016 book about the organization.[35] As Kirk wrote in a foreword to another book by another author in 2022, the campaign was so successful that the phrase "found its way into the American political lexicon."[36]

Johnson's tenure at Turning Point pushed the organization into a more targeted culture war. He helped Turning Point "own the libs" by mocking them. This is how Turning Point defines success on the mountain of entertainment. In this way, Johnson and Turning Point see memes as not merely entertainment; they are the "new front" in the culture war. A successful Turning Point meme by its own internal standards is "measured in the cutting commentary and the exposure."[37]

The phrase "Own the libs" is a cultural meme that seemingly originated in 2015, though it became viral during the 2016 election and the Trump administration that followed. By 2018 Trump's ambassador to the United Nations was criticizing Turning Point and Kirk at its own event for promoting the phrase to college students.[38] That didn't deter Johnson or Kirk. Turning Point took on the persona of its biggest supporter, Trump. As the conservative *Washington Examiner* wrote in 2018 in a profile of Kirk called "Kid Trump," "If the Young America's Foundation, or YAF, represents the older, pen-and-paper conservative order of William F. Buckley Jr. and Ronald Reagan then TPUSA codifies the new—the emotive, populist, and in-the-moment qualities of social media and Trump."[39]

The title of this chapter, "The Left Can't Meme," is a common claim by Johnson and the name of his Parler-exclusive show, which he began in 2022. While there is some truth to that, Johnson omits how his career as a conservative social media provocateur is a response to the internet activism of the left before the rise of social media. In fact, the "online right" adapted tactics of what one history of internet activism called the "Atheist Era" in the early 2000s. That era included, for the left's atheists such as Christopher Hitchens, "political strategies of superficial skepticism, 'owning' political opponents and labeling political opponents as hysterical and cringe." And once the "online right" began their internet response, "the online left was essentially relegated to a period of cultural inferiority for at least five years."[40] This is when Johnson started his career. By 2014 one scholar of digital media noted that "conservatives and authoritarian powers were seizing control of the digital space."[41] One study of more than two billion social media posts in 2016 and 2017 showed that "the most trafficked memes start on right-wing internet forums."[42]

Johnson's style is passed on to Turning Point acolytes during trainings at annual conferences and campus visits. Often before an adoring crowd, Johnson lays out his reason for not merely creating memes but consuming them. In a visit to a high school in Iowa as part of the Turning Point "Made in America" tour, Johnson described the effect of memes on gun owners: "It validates you. It fulfills you. . . . It lets you know you are not alone." Memes about the Second Amendment specifically fight back against those who "want to slander you, to make you feel like a bad person because you own firearms." But "memes can actually break through" that narrative, "more than anything else in the vertically integrated DNC apparatus of corporate media." Then Johnson played a clip from a Democratic politician who said he would "take away" AR-15s. That was followed by several clips of real and fictional people firing guns big and small set to fast-paced, hard-buzzing music. Johnson then said "they," aka the Democrats, hate memes.[43] Johnson told another tour that "ridicule is my weapon."[44]

Johnson said in the first episode of his Parler show that he creates memes "because memes hurt their [Democrats'] feelings." They are the "extremely fragile, sad, miserable cat-loving people who just want to wreck and ruin comedy for the rest of us." In other words, "Ridicule and make fun of the people you are not supposed to make fun of." During the 10-minute episodes Johnson appears in a blue-outlined box at the top of the screen, reacting to memes with his audience.[45] It's hard to know how many viewers each episode got. A July 2022 promo for the show on Parler's YouTube got nearly half a million views.[46] But Parler, which started in 2018, was removed "from Apple's and Google's app stores after the deadly January 6 riot at the Capitol, due to the site's inability or unwillingness to remove posts encouraging violence and crime."[47] While Parler was sold and eventually reinstated to app stores, the link of the feed for his show that Johnson posted to social media is no longer active as of September 2024.

This inspiration of hatred is the stated goal for Johnson and his memes. During September 2024, a false story began circulating about Haitian immigrants in Ohio. Memes about the story began going viral on conservative social media. According to *New York* magazine, "The story originated from white-supremacist sites online, which relentlessly promote the idea that non-white immigrants are dirty and dangerous. It quickly worked its way from the far right into mainstream conservative channels. Republicans seemed to think the idea gave them a potent meme."[48] Donald Trump mentioned the false story in his debate with Vice President Kamala Harris on September 10. Kirk also shared the story on his national radio show. A congressional hearing that same week also turned into a referendum on those memes. Johnson posted on social media a video clip from that hearing where a Democratic congressman was assailing the memes and the GOP chairman of the House committee who posted one. Johnson's post read, "How do we know we are winning? Democrats are losing their minds over memes in the halls of Congress."

When Memes Turned on Kirk

While Johnson and Turning Point have created their reputation through viral memes, when it doesn't work, especially when Turning Point itself has become fodder for memes, it is instructive to look at the organization's response. While Johnson preaches the enjoyment of making liberals lose their minds, Turning Point has been quick to disavow its own supporters who make it look bad. To conquer the mountain of entertainment means never becoming the subject of ridicule.

In October 2017, a campus chapter of Turning Point at Kent State University performed a demonstration during "Free Speech Week" that "featured one student dressed in a diaper, sucking on a pacifier in a playpen. The stunt was meant to mock the idea of 'safe spaces,' or protected areas on campus for marginalized groups, by symbolizing that only a baby would need one."[49] A photographer took several photos of the demonstration, which remain online. Those photos show an adult man wearing a diaper and a yellow shirt, sucking on a pacifier while using a pink crayon to draw in a coloring book. The "playpen" is a plastic fence, and on its outside is a Turning Point poster headlined "Your Censorship Offends Me."

The diaper event was derided again and again on social media. When Turning Point started a sister organization in Britain in 2019, a diaper meme followed. Even in 2024 an online search can find images of Kirk in a diaper, and some people on social media continue to fuel the myth that it was Kirk in the playpen. The immediate online backlash was so severe just a day after the event that Turning Point condemned it, saying it crossed a line into "the very obscure and inappropriate." It also claimed the event was not approved by anyone in Turning Point above the campus level.[50] The Kent State chapter disbanded, the chapter leader was removed from her position, and the mocking of Turning Point's event has continued for years. Even a fellow conservative group for college students mocked Turning Point for the event months later and added in a memo to its supporters that Turning Point had lied about its impact and growth.[51]

What was most ironic about the online response to the Turning Point diaper event was that it reappropriated a Turning Point meme to mock the organization. Just days before the October 18 event, Kirk posted a picture of himself with his hands on his hips. The image was accompanied by a list of claims often used by Turning Point, such as "Taxes are theft." It is Kirk's own photo of himself that is often modified to include a diaper.

Entertaining Our Democracy to Death

In Neil Postman's famous 1985 book *Amusing Ourselves to Death*, he wrote that "our politics, religion, news, athletics, education, and commerce have been transformed into congenial adjuncts of show business," and by always looking for amusement in social and cultural institutions, we are killing our nation.[52]

Not coincidentally, the areas listed by Postman are also the areas of cultural influence pushed by the seven mountains mandate movement. These have long been the pillars of a culture. His choice of amusement as our national disease may seem tame after decades of culture wars. But his conclusion about national death remains as powerful as ever. Entertainment as outrage, sports and pop culture as weapons, and the distracting division of internet culture is killing America. Turning Point as heir to the seven mountains movement thinks that to resurrect the nation as a Christian one, its current embodiment needs to die. And it is not only willing but backed by millions of dollars and eager influencers to strike a fatal blow at what it sees are the centers of a demonic kingdom. To have any chance of stopping the success of the Turning Point doctrine, we must stop seeing politics as entertainment and instead see our democracy as a culture of community.

Afterword

While Turning Point is a powerful organization, as a Christian nationalism agent it is not new. What makes it unique is not its origin in youth organizing (as that echoes Bill Bright and Loren Cunningham's religious efforts), but its pursuit of all seven mountains at once. While that frames it as the boldest organization in the history of the seven mountains mandate, it also means it is repeating actions and rhetoric we have heard before. And while this book is the first to display in detail the plans of Charlie Kirk and Turning Point, it is not the first to describe the impact of Christian nationalism on America. It is helpful to look back to others who aimed to tackle this ideology for help now with a new, though more virulent, strain of it.

For decades, the answer to the question of response—Where do reasonable Americans go from here?—has been answered nearly identically. One example will suffice. In 1995 a group of journalists and activists taking the title the Blue Mountain Working Group published a strategy document as part of a larger collection about Christian nationalism. That document urged the nation to turn its attention to the "anti-democratic right," which "seeks to control what we read, the music we hear, the images we see, how we learn," and other practices of culture. In response, the group pushed for the rest of us to defend pluralism, especially maintaining the separation of church and state through "broad popular coalitions" that include "all persons of good conscience willing to defend democratic pluralism," those who oppose authoritarian, theocratic rule, and "all persons who are willing to stand up for a real, dynamic, and vibrant democracy."[1]

The nation now faces not merely a new generation of this antidemocratic right with a well-funded heir with big dreams and immense power but also a president who understands how to take hold of American society through those seven divinely approved areas.

The stakes are higher for the nation and especially for Christians in America. What might millions of them like me do? Another return to the past is helpful. In 1992 a respected evangelical historian named Bruce Barron ended his book on dominion theology with a mild criticism. Barron said the plan to take each of the seven mountains "may be the pride that precedes a fall."[2] That gentle rebuke was paired with a warning of "dominionist disillusionment" to come. If "takeover rhetoric" was not followed by success, if the movement continued to "go overboard in its unyielding antagonism to non-Christian cultural forces" and not show results, at some point the hope born in such a movement might completely turn to rage. The future would be ominous.

Even with Trump in office for a second time, we could still see that disillusionment. After he leaves office, what shall we do with our brothers and sisters in Christ? With ourselves? With the gospel?

This will not be the last book on Christian nationalism, nor the last to pay attention to Turning Point. Both are poised for long-term impact.

The only way out is through. We must create communities, road by road, church by church, that sustain the elements of democracy.

Acknowledgments

While the bulk of this book was written in 2024, I first came across many of the themes and people mentioned in it as far back as the 1990s when I was a high school student. That was due to a man who happened to live behind my family in Augusta, Georgia. His name is Michael Pascarella.

I acknowledge the deep impact that he as a teacher and scholar had on this book. Soon he will be awarded a doctorate in education, a journey of sainthood.

I acknowledge my wife, Meg, and our two daughters, Nora and Miriam. Without them, I would have written a worse book, as I would have been a worse person. All of them are saints.

I acknowledge my parents. I acknowledge all my siblings. There are saints among us whom we call family.

I acknowledge my literary agent, Bridget Wagner Matzie, and her team at Aevitas. She was the first champion of this book and of me. She's a saint through and through.

I acknowledge my editor, Jessica Miller Kelley, and her team at Westminster John Knox. Jessica was always an encouraging voice as I wrote.

I acknowledge the wonderful education I received in the University of Florida's journalism program and the creative writing and rhetoric programs at the University of South Carolina.

I acknowledge my colleagues in the English department at the University of North Georgia who shared their excitement for this project.

I acknowledge the many other saints who have attended church with me, ministered with me, and loved me. They are a cloud of witnesses. Among that cloud is the monk Thomas Merton, who once wrote that our vocation is to work with God in the creation of our own life, an active participation in a freedom that chooses truth.

I acknowledge this book as an endeavor of truth-seeking.

Notes

Introduction

1. Loren Cunningham, *Winning God's Way* (YWAM Publishing, 1988), 123. Other accounts of this meeting can be found at https://ywam.org/legacy-word-2-discipling-nations-through-the-spheres-of-influence and https://www.youtube.com/watch?v=YuTmx2fJOxc.
2. Cunningham had a slightly different version of the list in *Winning God's Way*: "the home, the church, the schools, government and politics, the media, arts, entertainment and sports, and commerce, science, and technology."
3. Jack Jenkins, "New Study Finds Christian Nationalists to Be More Complex Than Media Portrayals," Religion News Service, December 18, 2023, https://religionnews.com/2023/12/18/new-study-paints-complicated-picture-of-christian-nationalists; Yonat Shimron, "Poll: A Third of Americans Are Christian Nationalists and Most Are White Evangelicals," Religion News Service, February 8, 2023, https://religionnews.com/2023/02/08/a-third-of-americans-are-christian-nationalists-and-most-are-white-evangelicals.
4. Paul Djupe, "Belief in the 7 Mountain Mandate Appears to Be Growing in the Last Year," May 13, 2024, https://religioninpublic.blog/2024/05/13/belief-in-the-7-mountain-mandate-appears-to-be-growing-in-the-last-year.
5. Matthew Taylor and Paul Djupe, "How Trumpism Has Pushed a Fringe Charismatic Theology into the Mainstream," Religion News Service, May 6, 2024, https://religionnews.com/2024/05/06/how-trumpism-has-pushed-a-fringe-charismatic-theology-into-the-mainstream.
6. https://www.baptistpress.com/wp-content/uploads/2022/05/2022-National-Day-of-Prayer-Guide.pdf.

7. Katherine Stewart, "What's Missing from Popular Discussions of Today's Christian Nationalism?" *Religion Dispatches*, August 9, 2021, https://religiondispatches.org/important-developments-weve-been-missing-about-todays-christian-nationalism.
8. "One Leader under God: The Connection between Authoritarianism and Christian Nationalism in America," PRRI, September 10, 2024, https://www.prri.org/research/one-leader-under-god-the-connection-between-authoritarianism-and-christian-nationalism-in-america/?preview=true.
9. "Support for Christian Nationalism in All 50 States: Findings from PRRI's 2023 American Values Atlas," PRRI, February 8, 2024, https://www.prri.org/research/support-for-christian-nationalism-in-all-50-states.
10. "Tracing the Rise of Christian Nationalism, from Trump to the Ala. Supreme Court," *Fresh Air*, February 29, 2024, https://www.npr.org/2024/02/29/1234843874/tracing-the-rise-of-christian-nationalism-from-trump-to-the-ala-supreme-court.
11. "Charlie Kirk Speaks at 2020 CPAC: Full Video," News 19 WLTX, February 27, 2020, https://www.youtube.com/watch?v=c-WiaPPxIHc.
12. Brian Slodysko, "How Trump's MAGA Movement Helped a 29-Year-Old Activist Become a Millionaire," Associated Press, October 10, 2023, https://apnews.com/article/election-2024-trump-turning-point-maga-d08a98e439fa4e902cb756d7e35153db.
13. https://www.documentcloud.org/documents/21091980-turning-point-usa-2021-investor-prospectus.
14. Djupe, "Belief in the 7 Mountain Mandate."
15. Mike Hixenbaugh and Allan Smith, "Charlie Kirk Once Pushed a 'Secular Worldview.' Now He's Fighting to Make America Christian Again," NBC News, June 12, 2024, https://www.nbcnews.com/politics/2024-election/charlie-kirk-turning-point-donald-trump-christian-nationalism-rcna156565.
16. https://www.facebook.com/watch/?v=628668922614238.
17. Steven Patrick Miller, *The Age of Evangelicalism: America's Born-Again Years* (Oxford University Press, 2014), 5; Cunningham, *Winning God's Way*, 121.
18. https://www.nae.org/youth-1970.
19. "An Evangelical Youth Event Could Offer Clues about the Movement's Future," *Washington Post*, June 24, 2022, https://www.washingtonpost.com/outlook/2022/06/24/an-evangelical-youth-event-could-offer-clues-about-movements-future.
20. Cunningham, *Winning God's Way*, 123.
21. Jeff Franklin, "Of Gates, Spheres, and Mountains," *Weekly Word*, November 26, 2012, https://weeklyword.eu/en/of-gates-spheres-and-mountains.
22. Robert Liebman and Robert Wuthnow, *The New Christian Right: Mobilization and Legitimation* (Aldine Publishing, 1983), 51.
23. https://pinnacleforum.com/about.

24. John G. Turner, *Bill Bright and Campus Crusade for Christ: The Renewal of Evangelicalism in Postwar America* (University of North Carolina Press, 2008), 324.
25. Bill Bright with Ron Jenson, *Kingdoms at War* (Here's Life Publishers, 1986), 7 and 17.
26. Mark Oppenheimer, "Son of Evangelical Royalty Turns His Back, and Tells the Tale," *New York Times*, August 19, 2011, https://www.nytimes.com/2011/08/20/us/20beliefs.html.
27. Kenneth Woodward, "Guru of Fundamentalism," *Newsweek*, November 1, 1982.
28. Charles Cotherman, *To Think Christianly: A History of L'Abri, Regent College, and the Christian Study Center Movement* (InterVarsity Press, 2020), 28.
29. Daniel K. Williams, *God's Own Party: The Making of the Christian Right* (Oxford University Press, 2010), 141.
30. Seth Dowland, "'Family Values' and the Formation of a Christian Right Agenda," *Church History* 78, no. 3 (2009): 606–31.
31. Francis Schaeffer, *The Christian Manifesto* (Crossway Books, 1981), 21.
32. Schaeffer, *Christian Manifesto*, 101.
33. Anna Garlin Spencer, "Marriage and Social Control," *Harvard Theological Review* 7, no. 3 (2011): 322.
34. *Encyclopedia of Education*, vol. 7, ed. James Guthrie (Macmillan, 1971), 434.
35. "Form and Freedom in the Church," July 23, 1974, https://lausanne.org/content/form-and-freedom-in-the-church.
36. William Edgar, "The Passing of R. J. Rushdoony," *First Things*, August 2001, https://www.firstthings.com/article/2001/08/the-passing-of-r-j-rushdoony.
37. Sara Diamond, *Spiritual Warfare* (South End Press, 1989), 206.
38. R. J. Rushdoony, *This Independent Republic* (Ross House Books, 2001), 138.
39. Francis Schaeffer, *Pollution and the Death of Man* (Tyndale House, 1970), 59.
40. C. Peter Wagner, *Church Growth and the Whole Gospel: A Biblical Mandate* (Harper & Row, 1981), 13.
41. *Christian Nationalism and the January 6th, 2021 Insurrection* (Baptist Joint Committee for Religious Liberty, 2022), 14.
42. https://lancewallnau.com/the-mountain-of-me.
43. Tim Dickinson, "Christian Nationalists Team Up on Illicit Push to Get Churches to Campaign for Trump," *Rolling Stone*, January 17, 2024, https://www.rollingstone.com/politics/politics-features/christian-nationalists-churches-campaign-trump-charlie-kirk-1234947887.
44. One such donor was Foster Friess, a long-time Republican donor from Wyoming, who became the group's first donor. It is no coincidence that Friess had been profiled in a 2001 book about successful Christian businessmen. Bright wrote the foreword to the book, saying he hoped "their example will rub off on the rest of us and society will be changed" through more generosity.

See Merrill J. Oster and Mike Hamel, *The Entrepreneur's Creed: The Principles and Passions of 20 Successful Entrepreneurs* (Broadman & Holman, 2001), xii.
45. "The Rubin Report," January 18, 2018, https://www.youtube.com/watch?v=FhCKfxy83BQ.
46. https://politicalresearch.org/2022/01/28/ten-years-turning-point-usa.
47. Natalie Allison, "How Turning Point, Once Spurned by the RNC, Is Becoming Trump's 'Force Multiplier' in Battleground States," June 15, 2024, https://www.politico.com/news/2024/06/15/turning-point-trump-battleground-states-00163563.
48. Ali Breland, "The Right's New Kingmaker," *Atlantic*, November 4, 2011, https://www.theatlantic.com/technology/archive/2024/11/charlie-kirk-turning-point-usa-kingmaker/680534.
49. "How We Win—LIVE from Godspeak Calvary Chapel," August 29, 2021, https://omny.fm/shows/the-charlie-kirk-show/how-we-win-live-from-godspeak-calvary-chapel.

Chapter 1: God's 1776 Project

1. "EPIC: Charlie Kirk Blasts Arizona School Board!" August 28, 2021, https://www.youtube.com/watch?v=r2LUlZkNRFs.
2. Julie Ingersoll, *Building God's Kingdom* (Oxford University Press, 2015), 79, 98, 80.
3. Michele Moorlag, "Principled Pluralism: Kuyper's Vision for Education and Its Relevance for the 21st Century," Abraham Kuyper Center, February 17, 2021, https://abrahamkuypercenter.nl/principled-pluralism-kuypers-vision-for-education-and-its-relevance-for-the-21st-century/.
4. Sara Diamond, *Spiritual Warfare* (South End Press, 1989), 85.
5. Andrew Torba and Andrew Isker, *Christian Nationalism: A Biblical Guide for Taking Dominion and Discipling Nations* (self-published, 2022), quoted in Bonnie Kristian, "Left Behind at the Ballot Box," *Christianity Today*, June 12, 2023, https://www.christianitytoday.com/ct/2023/july-august/politics-eschatology-vote-second-coming-nationalism.html.
6. Bright and Ron Jenson, *Kingdoms at War: Tactics for Victory in Nine Spiritual War Zones* (Here's Life Publishers, 1986), 158–61.
7. Johnny Enlow, *The Seven Mountain Prophecy* (Creation House, 2008), 84.
8. John Keilman, "Before Trump and Kanye Became Fans, Charlie Kirk Battled 'Marxist' High School Teachers in Chicago's Suburbs," October 22, 2018, https://www.chicagotribune.com/2018/10/22/before-trump-and-kanye-became-fans-charlie-kirk-battled-marxist-high-school-teachers-in-chicagos-suburbs.
9. Charlie Kirk, "BREAKING: Charlie Kirk Stands alongside Moms RISING UP against Scottsdale's School Board for Spying on Parents and Children," May 6, 2022, https://www.tpusa.com/live/breaking-charlie-kirk-stands

-alongside-moms-rising-up-against-scottsdales-school-board-for-spying-on-parents-and-children.
10. Tyler Kingkade, "Conservatives Are Changing K–12 Education, and One Christian College Is at the Center," July 20, 2023, https://www.nbcnews.com/news/us-news/hillsdale-college-1776-curriculum-k12-education-conservative-rcna93397.
11. Marta Aldrich, "Tennessee Charter Panel Leader Backs Five School Appeals, Including One from Hillsdale Group," October 2, 2023, https://www.chalkbeat.org/tennessee/2023/10/2/23899238/tennessee-charter-school-appeals-hillsdale-american-classical-education-memphis-nashville.
12. https://online.hillsdale.edu/landing/american-citizenship-and-its-decline; https://online.hillsdale.edu/landing/american-left; https://online.hillsdale.edu/landing/civil-rights-in-american-history.
13. "The 1776 Report," President's Advisory 1776 Commission, January 2021, National Archives, https://trumpwhitehouse.archives.gov.
14. "Looking to Understand American Politics in 2021? Aristotle's Got Answers," *Human Events*, March 9, 2021, https://humanevents.com/2021/03/09/looking-to-understand-american-politics-in-2021-aristotles-got-answers.
15. "Calling Out the Church—Part 1," Dobson Digital Library, James Dobson Family Institute, August 18, 2020, https://dobsonlibrary.com/resource/article/868d75d7-9bdc-4c6e-80ef-ddcfae69d2fb.
16. "Parents Need to Learn the Truth about Public Schools, ft. Hutz Hertzberg," https://www.youtube.com/watch?app=desktop&v=AH9JPvtelWA.
17. https://christianheritage.org/about/guiding-principles.
18. "Dr. Hutz Hertzberg, Pastor Summit," https://www.youtube.com/watch?v=HxDNNRW6NiA.
19. https://www.vintage.academy/a-5-c-school.
20. "Why Are We Starting a School; Vintage Academy," https://www.youtube.com/watch?v=1P7Y5MqVKo8&t=14s.
21. "Winning the 16,000 Hour War; Vintage Christian Academy," https://www.youtube.com/watch?v=El4iUGCLuJE&t=1s.
22. "The Babylonian Exile: Parents, Education, and Public Schools; 'Under God' Week Seven." https://www.youtube.com/watch?v=YGQxReyZGNY.
23. Warren Throckmorton, "The Popular Bonhoeffer Quote That Isn't in Bonhoeffer's Works," August 25, 2016, https://wthrockmorton.com/2016/08/25/the-popular-bonhoeffer-quote-that-isnt-in-bonhoeffers-works.
24. https://baptistnews.com/article/bonhoeffer-family-and-scholars-warn-against-metaxas-and-christian-nationalists.
25. https://www.schoolboardwatchlist.org.
26. Elizabeth Steiner, Heather Schwartz, and Melissa Kay Diliberti, "Educators' Poor Morale Matters, Even if They Don't Quit. Here's Why," The74Million.org, August 8, 2022, https://www.the74million.org/article/educators-poor-morale-matters-even-if-they-dont-quit-heres-why.

27. https://www.edchoice.org/school-choice/types-of-school-choice/what-are-school-vouchers-2/.
28. "Let's Talk about Education and School Choice in 2020," *The Hill*, May 16, 2019, https://thehill.com/opinion/education/443514-lets-talk-about-education-and-school-choice-in-2020.
29. Casey Tolan, Rene Marsh, and Nelli Black, "Arizona Is Sending Taxpayer Money to Religious Schools—and Billionaires See It as a Model for the US," June 19, 2024, https://www.cnn.com/2024/06/19/politics/arizona-private-school-vouchers-invs/index.html.
30. Kiera Butler, "Christian Nationalists Are Opening Private Schools. Taxpayers Are Funding Them," *Mother Jones*, June 17, 2024, https://www.motherjones.com/politics/2024/06/christian-nationalists-are-opening-private-schools-taxpayers-are-funding-them.
31. Mark Lieberman, "Most Students Getting New School Choice Funds Aren't Ditching Public Schools," *EducationWeek*, October 3, 2023, https://www.edweek.org/policy-politics/most-students-getting-new-school-choice-funds-arent-ditching-public-schools/2023/10.
32. "Arizona Faces Sweeping Budget Cuts, Driven by Flat Tax and Private School Vouchers," Center on Budget and Policy Priorities, July 2, 2024, https://www.cbpp.org/blog/arizona-faces-sweeping-budget-cuts-driven-by-flat-tax-and-private-school-vouchers.
33. "A Sharp Turn Right," July 2023, https://networkforpubliceducation.org/topics/reports.
34. https://k12.hillsdale.edu/About/Classical-Education.
35. https://www.tpusa.com/academy.
36. https://www.turningpointacademy.com/association.
37. https://www.turningpointacademy.com/resources.
38. https://www.apologia.com/shop/biology-3rd-edition-student-textbook.
39. https://bereanbuilders.com/ecomm/product/discovering-design-with-chemistry.
40. "Denial and Affirmation Four," Evangelical Free Church of America, March 12, 2024, https://www.efca.org/denial-and-affirmation-four.
41. Lexi Solomon, "NC Pastor Escorted from Wake School Board Meeting in Handcuffs. Was It a Publicity Stunt?" *Raleigh News and Observer*, October 5, 2024, https://www.newsobserver.com/news/local/education/article293446574.html#storylink=cpy.
42. Brahm Resnik, "TPUSA Employees Admit Guilt in Confrontation with Queer Instructor at Arizona State University, Court Documents Show," KPNX, April 23, 2024, https://www.12news.com/article/news/local/valley/tpusa-employees-court-ordered-diversion-program-harassing-queer-asu-educator/75-46a2401a-763b-4964-b3ae-d450442ec8b7; AZFamily Digital News Staff, "Charges Filed against

Two 'Turning Point USA' Members Accused of Harassing ASU Professor," KPHO TV, November 30, 2023, https://www.azfamily.com/2023/12/01/charges-filed-against-two-turning-point-usa-individuals-accused-harassing-asu-professor.
43. TJ L'Heureux, "2 Turning Point 'Bullies' Charged in Assault of Queer ASU Professor," *Phoenix New Times*, December 1, 2023, https://www.phoenixnewtimes.com/news/2-turning-point-bullies-charged-in-assault-of-queer-asu-professor-17670601.
44. Ryan Quinn, "Arizona State Instructor Followed, Injured by Turning Point USA Crew," October 14, 2023, https://www.insidehighered.com/news/faculty-issues/diversity-equity/2023/10/14/arizona-state-instructor-followed-injured-turning.
45. Johnny Enlow, *The Seven Mountain Prophecy* (Creation House, 2008), 81.
46. Bill Bright and Ron Jenson, *Kingdoms at War: Tactics for Victory in Nine Spiritual War Zones* (Here's Life, 1986), 163–64.
47. Owen Strachan, "Bill Bright and Campus Crusade for Christ," Gospel Coalition, June 23, 2011, https://www.thegospelcoalition.org/reviews/bill-bright.
48. Keri Ladner, "The Quiet Rise of Christian Dominionism," *Christian Century*, November 2022, https://www.christiancentury.org/article/features/quiet-rise-christian-dominionism.

Chapter 2: Counselor to the King

1. Steve Benen, "Marjorie Taylor Greene Talks Up 'National Divorce' (Yes, Again)," MSNBC, January 29, 2024, https://www.msnbc.com/rachel-maddow-show/maddowblog/marjorie-taylor-greene-talks-national-divorce-yes-rcna136234.
2. "Does America Need a National Divorce? With Rep. Marjorie Taylor Greene and Julaine Appling," *The Charlie Kirk Show*, February 22, 2023, https://thecharliekirkshow.com/podcasts/the-charlie-kirk-show/does-america-need-a-national-divorce-with-rep-marj.
3. Matthew Boedy, "Charlie Kirk and Other Young Conservatives Are Increasingly Embracing Identity Politics," *Flux*, April 26, 2021, https://flux.community/matthew-boedy/2021/04/previously-republican-states-start-voting-democratic-right-becoming-decidedly.
4. Bradley Onishi and Matthew D. Taylor, "The Key to Mike Johnson's Christian Extremism Hangs outside His Office," *Rolling Stone*, November 10, 2023, https://www.rollingstone.com/politics/political-commentary/mike-johnson-christian-nationalist-appeal-to-heaven-flag-1234873851.
5. Loren Cunningham, *Winning God's Way* (YWAM Publishing, 1988), 132; Bill Bright and Ron Jenson, *Kingdoms at War: Tactics for Victory in Nine Spiritual War Zones* (Here's Life, 1986), 146.

6. R. J. Rushdoony, "Sphere Laws," in *Independent Republic* (Craig Press, 1964), quoted from condensed version available at https://chalcedon.edu/resources/articles/sphere-law.
7. "What Are Biblical Blueprints?" *Biblical Economics Today* 9, no. 6 (October/November 1986): 104, https://www.garynorth.com/public/14763.cfm.
8. Bob Smietana, "Old-School Christian Nationalism's Avatar of Racism, Antisemitism, and Conspiracies," Religion News Service, March 7, 2023, https://religionnews.com/2023/03/07/for-gerald-l-k-smith-old-school-christian-nationalism-meant-racism-antisemitism-and-conspiracies.
9. "Unreached Peoples: Recent Developments in the Concept," *Mission Frontiers*, August 1, 1989, https://www.missionfrontiers.org/issue/article/unreached-peoples.
10. https://ifapray.org/blog/fighting-spiritual-warfare-in-richmond-va.
11. Sarah Miller, "Soldiers for Christ: The History and Future of Dominionism in America," 2012, Honors Thesis Collection 22, Wellesley College, https://repository.wellesley.edu/thesiscollection/22.
12. Jane Lampman, "Targeting Cities with 'Spiritual Mapping,' Prayer," *Christian Science Monitor*, September 23, 1999, https://www.csmonitor.com/1999/0923/p15s1.html.
13. John Dawson, *Taking Our Cities for God* (Charisma House, 1989), 30.
14. "Pray," *This American Life*, September 26, 1997, https://www.thisamericanlife.org/77/pray.
15. Bruce Wilson, "Fighting Demons, Raising the Dead, Taking Over the World," *Religion Dispatches*, June 22, 2009, https://religiondispatches.org/fighting-demons-raising-the-dead-taking-over-the-world.
16. Jennifer Cohn, "Pennsylvania's Prayer Warrior," *Bucks County Beacon*, July 11, 2023, https://buckscountybeacon.com/2023/07/pennsylvanias-prayer-warrior-abby-abildness-and-her-dominionist-crusade-in-the-commonwealth.
17. https://www.newchristendompress.com/conference.
18. Marina Johnson, "'The Guardian' Calls It a 'Community for Rightwingers,'" *Louisville Courier-Journal*, January 22, 2024, https://www.courier-journal.com/story/news/local/2024/01/22/christian-residential-community-rural-kentucky-tennessee-appalachia-eastern-highland-rim/72309774007.
19. https://www.cityelders.com.
20. "Cracks on the Road to Christian Dominion: Is the Shadowy 'City Elders' Group Collapsing?" November 12, 2023, https://www.salon.com/2023/11/12/cracks-on-the-road-to-christian-dominion-is-the-shadowy-city-elders-group-collapsing.
21. Kyle Mantyla, "Oklahoma State Sen. Dusty Deevers Provides a Case Study in Christian Nationalism," Right Wing Watch, January 29, 2024, https://www.rightwingwatch.org/post/oklahoma-state-sen-dusty-deevers-provides-a-case-study-in-christian-nationalism.

22. Barry Hankins, *Francis Schaeffer and the Shaping of Evangelical America* (Wm. B. Eerdmans, 2008), 178.
23. William Wolfe, "When the Government Plays God: The Threat of 'Statism' to Christianity in America," Standing for Freedom Center, March 1, 2022, https://www.standingforfreedom.com/2022/03/when-the-government-plays-god-the-threat-of-statism-to-christianity-in-america.
24. "Resistance to Tyrants and Obedience to God," Blog and Mablog, February 13, 2023, https://dougwils.com/books-and-culture/books/resistance-to-tyrants-obedience-to-god.html
25. Paul D. Miller, "A Tale of Two Books, One Podcast, and the Contest over Christian Nationalism," *Christianity Today*, December 20, 2022, https://www.christianitytoday.com/ct/2022/december-web-only/stephen-wolfe-case-christian-nationalism-paul-miller.html.
26. Matthew Taylor, *The Violent Take It by Force* (Broadleaf Books, 2024), 164.
27. "Charlie Kirk Speaks at Colorado Christian Academy," Colorado Christian Academy, December 3, 2023, https://www.youtube.com/watch?v=KG1umuf5u1s.
28. Matthew Boedy, "Charlie Kirk Audience Member Asking 'When Do We Get to Use the Guns' Shows Where GOP Rhetoric Leads," *Flux*, October 28, 2021, https://flux.community/matthew-boedy/2021/10/charlie-kirk-audience-member-asking-when-do-we-get-use-guns-shows-how-gop.
29. "Charlie Kirk on Trump Surrender: 'Getting a Mug Shot, That's an Act of Violence,'" *Media Matters*, August 25, 2023, https://www.mediamatters.org/charlie-kirk/charlie-kirk-trump-surrender-getting-mug-shot-thats-act-violence.
30. City Elders, "Turning Point USA to City Elders 2.29.24," February 29, 2024, https://www.youtube.com/watch?v=eIfV6Q8bMWg.
31. "God and Government—The Law," Trinity Dallas, January 27, 2020, https://www.youtube.com/watch?v=nKgwDajgaOc.
32. "Charlie Kirk: America at a Turning Point—Part 2," Dr. James Dobson's Family Talk, August 19, 2020, https://familytalk.widen.net/s/rzyucdcj9j.
33. Turning Point USA, "Charlie Kirk: America Needs a Fifth Great Awakening," September 23, 2021, https://www.youtube.com/watch?v=bCehvDHpjHA.
34. David Brody, "Game-Changing Recipe for 2020? 'Pastors and Pews' Model to Motivate Christian Voters," August 8, 2019, https://cbn.com/news/politics/game-changing-recipe-2020-pastors-and-pews-model-motivate-christian-voters.
35. "Are We Preserving the Liberty to Win People to Christ?" *Charisma News*, April 12, 2023, https://charismanews.com/opinion/renewing-america/are-we-preserving-the-liberty-to-win-people-to-christ.
36. "Rumblings of Theocratic Violence," *Political Research Associates*, June 11, 2014, https://politicalresearch.org/2014/06/11/rumblings-of-theocratic-violence.

37. "Two Persecuted Pastors," *The Charlie Kirk Show*, August 9, 2020, https://www.happyscribe.com/public/the-charlie-kirk-show/two-persecuted-pastors-with-jack-hibbs-and-rob-mccoy.
38. Bruce Barron, *Heaven on Earth? The Social and Political Agendas of Dominion Theology* (Zondervan, 1992), 34.
39. Quoted in Rick Pidcock, "No, the U.S. Constitution Is Not Based on the Book of Deuteronomy," *Baptist News Global*, March 11, 2024, https://baptistnews.com/article/no-the-u-s-constitution-is-not-based-on-the-book-of-deuteronomy.

Chapter 3: Biblical Citizenship

1. Ethridge was not the only pastor arrested for actions that day. Brian Kaylor, "The J6 Pastors," *Word and Way*, January 4, 2024, https://wordandway.org/2024/01/04/the-j6-pastors.
2. Katherine Stewart, *The Power Worshippers: Inside the Dangerous Rise of Religious Nationalism* (Bloomsbury, 2020), 175.
3. David K. Naugle, "Worldview: History, Theology, Implications," lecture given at Cornerstone University, September 2004, https://www.leaderu.com/philosophy/worldviewhistory.html.
4. https://www.coalition-on-revival.net/documents.
5. D. James Kennedy, "Christian Citizenship," Coral Ridge Presbyterian Church, September 18, 1988, https://www.djameskennedy.com/full-view-sermon/djk18838a-christian-citizenship.
6. Lance Wallnau, "Marketplace Invasion," in *Transformational Coaching*, ed. Joseph Umidi (Xulon Press, 2005), 193–211.
7. Matthew Taylor, *The Violent Take It by Force* (Broadleaf, 2024), 151.
8. Johnny Enlow, *The Seven Mountain Mandate* (Creation House, 2008), 26.
9. "Fake Worldviews, and the True One: My Speech to the Texas Youth Summit," *The Charlie Kirk Show*, October 10, 2023.
10. "American Worldview Inventory 2024 (Release #3)," Cultural Research Center, May 28, 2024, https://www.arizonachristian.edu/wp-content/uploads/2024/05/CRC-Release-AWVI-3-May-28-2024.pdf.
11. "Charlie Kirk at the Pastor's Summit," June 2, 2023, https://www.youtube.com/watch?v=abvzRdlQyJ8&t=3s.
12. Nick Adams, *Ten Ways America Is the Greatest Country in the History of the World!* (Turning Point USA, 2015), https://cdn.tpusa.com/assets/books/10WaysAmericaIsTheGreatestCountry.pdf, 2.
13. "Charlie Kirk at The Pastor's Summit in Nashville, TN 2023 Day 1," June 2, 2023, https://www.youtube.com/watch?v=abvzRdlQyJ8&t=3s.
14. https://libertypastorsu.com.
15. https://www.declaration4liberty.com; it's unclear what Blair means by the ill of "suffrage."

16. Steven Monacelli, "The 'Remnant Alliance Is Coming for a School Board Near You," *Texas Observer*, May 8, 2024, https://www.texasobserver.org/christian-schoolboards-education-k12.
17. "Ridin' the Storm Out: Will the Next Crash Usher in CBDC? Charlie Kirk and Paul Blair Discuss," *Fairview Baptist Edmond*, 2024, https://rumble.com/v2mfpts-will-the-next-crash-usher-in-cbdc-charlie-kirk-and-paul-blair-discuss.html.
18. John Whittaker, "Review of Eric Metaxas's 'Letter to the American Church' the Movie," Renew Network, 2024, https://renew.org/review-letter-to-the-american-church-the-movie.
19. Katherine Hamilton, "Exclusive: Charlie Kirk Calls Out 'Cowardly' Churches Adopting Left-Wing Politics," Breitbart News, July 24, 2023, https://www.breitbart.com/politics/2023/07/24/charlie-kirk-calls-out-cowardly-churches-adopting-left-wing-politics.
20. Taylor, *Violent Take It by Force*, 86.
21. "Objectives and Outcomes," Wagner University, 2024, https://wagner.university/master-of-apostolic-leadership-and-applied-ministry.
22. "Is There a Revival in America?" October 17, 2023, https://www.youtube.com/watch?v=D6A6L9DrbsM.
23. Ché Ahn, *Say Goodbye to Powerless Christianity: Walking in Supernatural Surrender and Significance* (Destiny Image, 2009).
24. Kyle Mantyla, "Ché Ahn's Churches Are Funding Candidates Who'll Serve as 'The Legislative Body of the Kingdom of God,'" Right Wing Watch, March 22, 2024, https://www.peoplefor.org/rightwingwatch/post/che-ahns-churches-are-funding-candidates-wholl-serve-as-the-legislative-body-of-the-kingdom-of-god.
25. "Prayer Priorities for America: April 2019," April 1, 2019, https://blog.ronniefloyd.com/13723/america/prayer-priorities-for-america-april-2019-pray-for-the-7-centers-of-influence-in-america.
26. Mark Wingfield, "Conservative Baptist Network Got $50,000 from Far-Right Political Group Last Year," Baptist News Global, June 27, 2023, https://baptistnews.com/article/conservative-baptist-network-got-50000-from-far-right-political-group-last-year.
27. Bill Bright and Ron Jenson, *Kingdoms at War: Tactics for Victory in Nine Spiritual War Zones* (Here's Life, 1986), 113.
28. Laura Jedeed, "My Week inside a Right-Wing 'Constitutional Defense' Training Camp," *New Republic*, January 3, 2023, https://newrepublic.com/article/169563/patriot-academy-right-wing-constitutional-defense-training-camp.
29. Bob Smietana, "Phoenix Pastor a Missionary to Christian Nationalists," Religion News Service, November 14, 2022, https://www.baptiststandard.com/news/nation/phoenix-pastor-a-missionary-to-christian-nationalists.

30. "Thy Kingdom Come: Praying as Reformers," Generals International, https://www.generals.org/blog/thy-kingdom-come-praying-as-reformers.
31. John Fea, "Eric Metaxas Prepares Pastors for a Holy War," *Current*, September 14, 2023, https://currentpub.com/2023/09/14/eric-metaxas-prepares-pastors-for-a-holy-war.
32. Joseph Fronczak, "The Fascist Game: Transnational Political Transmission and the Genesis of the U.S. Modern Right," *Journal of American History* 105, no. 3 (December 2018): 563–88.
33. "The Fascist Game: A Conversation on the Origins of the American Modern Right," *Process: A Blog for American History*, 2024, https://www.oah.org/process-blog/fronczak-fascism.
34. Peter Wagner, *Dominion! How Kingdom Action Can Change the World* (Chosen Books, 2008), 14 and 144.
35. "Charlie Kirk: Practicing and Protecting Religious Freedom," Kirk Cameron on TBN, February 19, 2022, https://www.youtube.com/watch?v=gnK0RNdtqLI.
36. Mark Silk, "Does the Constitution Depend on Morality and Religion?" Religion News Service, January 16, 2024, https://religionnews.com/2024/01/16/does-the-constitution-depend-on-morality-and-religion.
37. Mantyla, "Ché Ahn's Churches.'"
38. Taylor, *Violent Take It by Force*, 216.
39. Rick Renner, "The Earliest Historical Use of the Word 'Church,'" Renner Ministries, 2024, https://renner.org/article/a-and-p-excerpt-1.
40. Oasis Church, "Deploy the Ekklesia—Greg Hood," June 18, 2023, https://www.youtube.com/watch?v=Rb0IxGSS8H4.
41. "Religious Freedom," Cross Assembly, November 1, 2020, https://crossassembly.org/media/v5hpm35/religious-freedom.
42. Kyle Mantyla, "Christian Nationalists Speak Openly about Weaponizing the Supreme Court to Install Theocracy," *Flux*, June 7, 2023, https://flux.community/kyle-mantyla/2023/06/christian-nationalists-speak-openly-about-weaponizing-the-supreme-court-to-install-theocracy.
43. Taylor, *Violent Take It by Force*, 216.
44. Bruce Barron, *Heaven on Earth? The Social and Political Agendas of Dominion Theology* (Zondervan, 1992), 113.
45. Hal Lindsey, *The Road to Holocaust* (Bantam, 1989), 25, quoted in Thomas D. Ice, "Hal Lindsey, Dominion Theology, and Anti-Semitism," Article Archives, Liberty University, 2009, https://digitalcommons.liberty.edu/pretrib_arch/49.
46. "TPUSA Stands with Israel," https://israel.tpusa.com.
47. Frederick Clarkson, "Christian Reconstructionism," in *Eyes Right! Challenging the Right Wing Backlash*, ed. Chip Berlet (South End Press, 1995), 70.
48. Tim Dickinson, "Turning Point USA's AmericaFest Is Infested with Antisemitism," *Rolling Stone*, December 16, 2023, https://www.rollingstone

.com/politics/politics-news/turning-point-usa-americafest-infested-antisemitism-1234930583.
49. Eboo Patel and Robert P. Jones, "What the History of 'Judeo-Christian' Can Teach Us about Fighting Christian Nationalism," InterFaith America, July 20, 2022, https://www.interfaithamerica.org/article/what-the-history-of-judeo-christian-can-teach-us-about-fighting-christian-nationalism.
50. "A Leading Figure in the New Apostolic Reformation," *Fresh Air*, October 3, 2011, https://www.npr.org/2011/10/03/140946482/apostolic-leader-weighs-religions-role-in-politics.
51. In *The Seven Mountain Prophecy*, Johnny Enlow wrote that Islam "may in fact be a manifestation of the Antichrist" (135).
52. "How Islam Really Views the West," *The Charlie Kirk Show*, May 14, 2024, https://thecharliekirkshow.com/podcasts/the-charlie-kirk-show/how-islam-really-views-the-west.
53. "Charlie Kirk: Practicing and Protecting Religious Freedom."
54. https://crossassembly.org/media/v5hpm35/religious-freedom.
55. Caleb Campbell, *Disarming Leviathan: Loving Your Christian Nationalist Neighbor* (InterVarsity Press, 2024), 8.
56. Taylor, *Violent Take It by Force*, 195.

Chapter 4: The Masculine Heart and the Feminine Mystique

1. "HPD Responds to Child Enticement Situation," September 13, 2023, https://www.cityofhastings.org/news/latest-news/2023/09/13/hpd-responds-to-child-enticement-situation.
2. "To Catch a Trans Pedophile with Kalen D'Almeida and Noel Fritsch," *The Charlie Kirk Show*, September 8, 2023. https://thecharliekirkshow.com/podcasts/the-charlie-kirk-show/to-catch-a-trans-pedophile-with-kalen-dalmeida-and.
3. "To Catch a Trans Pedophile."
4. "To Catch a Trans Pedophile."
5. Anya Zoledzlowski, "CPAC Speaker Calls for Eradication of 'Transgenderism,' Crowd Goes Wild," Vice, March 6, 2023, https://www.vice.com/en/article/bvjgnq/cpac-transgenderism-speaker-called-for-eradication; "Daily Wire Host: 'I Support Christian Nationalism,'" Media Matters, December 11, 2023, https://www.mediamatters.org/michael-knowles/daily-wire-host-i-support-christian-nationalism.
6. Kaylee McGhee, "Charlie Kirk and TPUSA Aren't Conservative, as Real Conservatives Already Knew," June 21, 2018, https://hillsdalecollegian.com/2018/06/charlie-kirk-tpusa-arent-conservative-real-conservatives-already-knew.
7. Alex Griffing, "Black, Gay Republican Tells CNN the 'Soulless Dead-Eyed White Supremacists' Harassing Him at MAGA Event 'Could Have Bashed My Brains In,'" Mediaite, December 20, 2023, https://www.mediaite.com

/tv/black-gay-republican-tells-cnn-the-soulless-dead-eyed-white-supremacists-harassing-him-at-maga-event-could-have-bashed-my-brains-in.
8. J. D. Wolf, "Trump Campaign Partner Charlie Kirk Called Being Gay an 'Error,' Praised Stoning to Death," MeidasTouch News, June 12, 2024, https://meidasnews.com/news/trump-campaign-partner-charlie-kirk-called-being-gay-an-error-praised-stoning-to-death.
9. Sara Diamond, *Not by Politics Alone* (Guilford Press, 1998), 166.
10. Kyle Mantyla, "Right Wing Bonus Tracks: A Throbbing Middle Finger to God," Right Wing Watch, September 11, 2023, https://www.rightwingwatch.org/post/right-wing-bonus-tracks-a-throbbing-middle-finger-to-god.
11. Diamond, *Not by Politics Alone*, 103.
12. "50 Years of Biblical Feminism: As Told by Letha Dawson Scanzoni," Christian Feminism Today, June 2014, https://eewc.com/letha-dawson-scanzoni-50-years-biblical-feminism.
13. Jessica Hong, "The Feminine Mystique at 50," September 13, 2013, https://www.thegospelcoalition.org/reviews/feminine-mystique-50.
14. Stu Weber, *Tender Warrior: God's Intention for a Man* (Multnomah Books, 1993), https://stuweber.com/tender-warrior.
15. John Eldredge, *Wild at Heart* (Thomas Nelson, 2001), 7.
16. https://www.youtube.com/watch?v=Am1tfdg3MwE.
17. Stephanie Pappas, "APA Issues First-Ever Guidelines for Practice with Men and Boys," *Monitor on Psychology* 50, no. 1 (2019): 34.
18. https://tpusafaith.com/men.
19. https://www.mensalliancetribe.com/about/leadership.
20. "Be a Man! With Spencer Mozingo," *The Charlie Kirk Show*, January 24, 2023, https://omny.fm/shows/the-charlie-kirk-show/be-a-man-with-spencer-mozingo.
21. https://www.tpusa.com/live/turning-point-usa-announces-young-womens-leadership-summit-2024.
22. Kara Voght, "Inside a Conservative Confab for Young Women, Where Feminism Is a Lie," *Washington Post*, June 15, 2023, https://www.washingtonpost.com/lifestyle/2023/06/15/inside-conservative-confab-young-women-where-feminism-is-lie.
23. https://www.tpusa.com/ywlslive/chaya-raichik-ywls2023-full-speech.
24. https://www.tpusa.com/ywlslive/erika-kirk-ywls2023-full-speech.
25. "Becoming the Guardian of Your Home with Erika Kirk," January 4, 2024, *Blessings and Motherhood*, https://blessingsandmotherhood.com/becoming-the-guardian-of-your-home.
26. John Turner, *Bill Bright and Campus Crusade for Christ: The Renewal of Evangelicalism in Postwar America* (University of North Carolina Press, 2009), 55–58.
27. Bill Bright and Ron Jenson, *Kingdoms at War: Tactics for Victory in Nine Spiritual War Zones* (Here's Life, 1986), 99, 101.

28. Loren Cunningham, *Why Not Women? A Fresh Look at Scripture on Women in Missions, Ministry, and Leadership* (YWAM, 2000), https://lorencunningham.com/books/episode-04-long-distance-b835l.
29. Quoted in F. A. S. Hornstra-Fuchs and W. L. Hornstra, "Female Leaders in an International Evangelical Mission Organisation: An Empirical Study of Youth with a Mission in Germany," *Koers* 75, no. 3 (2010): 589–611.
30. "Can a Woman Be a Woman? ft. Mrs. Erika Kirk—YWLS 2023," June 2, 2023, https://www.youtube.com/watch?v=K9Mlhbf0lWg.
31. Shobana Vetrivel, "Proverbs 31 Is for Everyone," Gospel Coalition, August 9, 2022, https://in.thegospelcoalition.org/article/proverbs-31-is-for-everyone.
32. "The Woman of Valor: A Fresh Look at Proverbs 31," Christians for Biblical Equality International, 2024, https://www.cbeinternational.org/resource/woman-valor-fresh-look-proverbs-31.
33. Bright and Jenson, *Kingdoms at War*, 107.
34. Mary Kassian, "Complementarianism for Dummies," Gospel Coalition, September 4, 2012, https://www.thegospelcoalition.org/article/complementarianism-for-dummies.
35. https://www.mrserikakirk.com/listen/episode/677e773b/vote.
36. "On YouTube, Charlie Kirk Calls for Men to Confront and Physically Prevent Trans Student Athletes from Competing," Media Matters, March 20, 2022, https://www.mediamatters.org/charlie-kirk/youtube-charlie-kirk-calls-men-confront-and-physically-prevent-trans-student-athletes.
37. "Tough Love with Charlie and Erika Kirk," *The Charlie Kirk Show*, September 24, 2023, https://thecharliekirkshow.com/podcasts/the-charlie-kirk-show/tough-love-with-charlie-and-erika-kirk.
38. "Who Killed Mars Hill?" *Christianity Today*, June 21, 2021, https://www.christianitytoday.com/ct/podcasts/rise-and-fall-of-mars-hill/who-killed-mars-hill-church-mark-driscoll-rise-fall.html.
39. Kevin DeYoung, "Death to the Patriarchy? Complementarity and the Scandal of 'Father Rule,'" Desiring God, July 19, 2022, https://www.desiringgod.org/articles/death-to-the-patriarchy.

Chapter 5: Marketplace Apostles in God's Economy

1. Pat Robertson, "Is Capitalism Right or Wrong?" CBN, https://www2.cbn.com/article/finances/capitalism-right-or-wrong.
2. Andy Kroll and Nick Surgey, "Inside Ziklag, the Secret Organization of Wealthy Christians Trying to Sway the Election and Change the Country," ProPublica, July 13, 2024, https://www.propublica.org/article/inside-ziklag-secret-christian-charity-2024-election.
3. "Charlie Kirk: 'Cryptocurrency and Christians . . . Are Two Threats to the New World Order,'" Media Matters, July 29, 2024, https://www.mediamatters.org/charlie-kirk/charlie-kirk-cryptocurrency-and-christians-are-two-threats-new-world-order.

4. "Charlie Kirk Reveals What the Bible REALLY Says about Money," 7 Figure Squad, September 5, 2023, https://www.youtube.com/watch?v=hi3ON0gU9lc.
5. Jennifer Kelly Geddes, "Turning Point USA Founder Charlie Kirk Is Selling His Scottsdale Mansion for $6.5M," Realtor.com, March 13, 2024, https://www.realtor.com/news/celebrity-real-estate/charlie-kirk-is-selling-his-scottsdale-arizona-mansion-for-6-5m.
6. Brian Slodysko, "How Trump's MAGA Movement Helped a 29-Year-Old Activist Become a Millionaire," Associated Press, October 10, 2023, https://apnews.com/article/election-2024-trump-turning-point-maga-d08a98e439fa4e902cb756d7e35153db.
7. Quoted in David Smith, "Candace Owens Woos the Right as Provocative Face of Trump Youth," *The Guardian*, March 2, 2019, https://www.theguardian.com/us-news/2019/mar/02/candace-owens-provocative-face-trump-youth.
8. "How the Free Market Trumps Socialism," *Washington Times*, September 17, 2019, https://www.washingtontimes.com/news/2019/sep/17/how-the-free-market-trumps-socialism.
9. Michael Wilkinson, "The Prosperity Gospel and the Globalization of American Capitalism," in *Religious Activism in the Global Economy*, ed. Peter J. Smith and Sabine Dreher (Rowman and Littlefield, 2016), 60.
10. Gloria Copeland, *God's Will Is Prosperity* (Copeland Publications, 1978), 82.
11. Quoted in Melanie Hemry, "Farmer and Fisher of Men," Believers Voice of Victory, September 2011, https://secure.kcm.org.au/wp-content/uploads/2011/09/au_mag_201109.pdf, 9.
12. Jay Van Andel, "Economic and Social Challenges of the Eighties," *Imprimis* 10, no. 6 (June 1981), https://imprimis.hillsdale.edu/economic-and-social-challenges-of-the-eighties.
13. John Avanzini, *The Wealth of the World* (Harrison House, 1989).
14. Pat Robertson, *The New World Order* (Word Publishing, 1991), 207.
15. https://strategic-initiatives.org/the-wealth-transfer-revisited.
16. Peter Wagner, *The Church in the Workplace* (Regal Books, 2006), 33.
17. Peter Wagner, "Stewarding for Reformation," in *The Reformer's Pledge*, ed. Che Ahn (Destiny Image, 2010), 196.
18. Elmer L. Towns, "Trends among Fundamentalists," July 6, 1973, https://www.christianitytoday.com/ct/1973/july-6.
19. Hamon, *The Eternal Church* (Destiny Image, 1981), 389.
20. Peter Wagner, *The Great Transfer of Wealth: Financial Release for Advancing God's Kingdom* (Whitaker House, 2014).
21. Dennis Peacocke, *Winning the Battle for Minds of Men* (Alive and Free, 1987), 3.
22. Dennis Peacocke, "Co-Managing the Earth: The Foundational Work of the Christian Marketplace Ministry," GoStrategic, https://www.gostrategic

.org/articles/co-managing-the-earth-the-foundational-work-of-the-christian-marketplace-ministry.

23. Lance Wallnau, "Marketplace Invasion: A Prophetic Call to Transforming the Workplace," in *Transformational Coaching*, ed. Joseph Umidi (Xulon Press, 2005), 204 and 209.
24. Kate Bowler, *Blessed: A History of the American Prosperity Gospel* (Oxford University Press, 2013), 7.
25. Edward Suh, *The Empowering God: Redeeming the Prosperity Movement and Overcoming Victim Trauma in the Poor* (Pickwick Publications, 2021), 4.
26. "Defeating the Poverty Mindset," CityLight Church, January 22, 2024, https://citylightnyc.com/defeating-the-poverty-mindset.
27. Don Johnson, "The Creation of Wealth and the Alleviation of Poverty," in *Daring to Live on the Edge*, by Loren Cunningham (YWAM Publishing, 1991), 197.
28. Shayne Lee and Phillip Luke Sinitiere, *Holy Mavericks: Evangelical Innovators and the Spiritual Marketplace* (NYU Press, 2009), 99.
29. "Don't Dwell on the Past, Don't Be a Victim," TPUSA Live, October 2, 2022, https://www.tpusa.com/live/dont-dwell-on-the-past-dont-be-a-victim.
30. "You Deserve Better Than the Victim Mentality," TPUSA Live, March 4, 2022, https://www.tpusa.com/live/you-deserve-better-than-the-victim-mentality.
31. Rebecca Nelson, "Candace Owens Is the New Face of Black Conservatism," *Washington Post*, March 6, 2019, https://www.washingtonpost.com/news/magazine/wp/2019/03/06/feature/candace-owens-is-the-new-face-of-black-conservatism-but-what-does-that-really-mean.
32. "Steamboat Institute Freedom Conference 2018," August 11, 2018, https://www.c-span.org/video/?448631-1/steamboat-institute-freedom-conference.
33. Kelly Weill, "Blexit's Finances Are Slumping—but Its Paycheck to Candace Owens Keeps Coming," *Daily Beast*, October 28, 2022, https://www.thedailybeast.com/blexits-finances-are-slumpingbut-its-paycheck-to-candace-owens-keeps-coming/?source=articles&via=rss.
34. https://www.blexit.com/libraries/financial-literacy.
35. Amanda Cuda, "We Were Children. I Wasn't the Only Victim," *Connecticut Post*, March 5, 2016, https://www.ctpost.com/local/article/We-were-children-I-wasn-t-the-only-6872580.php.
36. Brandy Zadrozny, "YouTube Tested, Trump Approved: How Candace Owens Suddenly Became the Loudest Voice on the Far Right," NBC News, June 23, 2018, https://www.nbcnews.com/news/us-news/youtube-tested-trump-approved-how-candace-owens-suddenly-became-loudest-n885166.
37. Carolyn Moxley Rouse, John L. Jackson, and Marla Frederick, *Televised Redemption: Black Religious Media and Racial Empowerment* (NYU Press, 2016), 122.

38. "God Picks People to Have Experiences in Their Lives—Both Good and Bad," October 3, 2022, https://www.youtube.com/watch?v=xr1jFAdGWN4.
39. Jacinta Render, "Rep. Ted Lieu Plays Clip of Candace Owens' Hitler Comments at Hearing on White Nationalism," ABC News, April 9, 2019, https://abcnews.go.com/ABCNews/repted-lieu-plays-clip-candace-owens-hitler-comments/story?id=62286256.
40. Jared Holt, "Turning Point USA Chapters Call for Candace Owens' Expulsion," Right Wing Watch, February 21, 2019, https://www.peoplefor.org/rightwingwatch/post/turning-point-usa-chapters-call-for-candace-owens-expulsion.
41. Oliver Darcy, "Ben Shapiro's the Daily Wire Severs Ties with Candace Owens after Her Embrace of Antisemitic Rhetoric," CNN, March 22, 2024, https://www.cnn.com/2024/03/22/media/candace-owen-out-ben-shapiro-daily-wire-anti-semitism/index.html.
42. "Goodbye Candace," *FrontPage Magazine*, November 20, 2023, https://www.frontpagemag.com/goodbye-candace.
43. https://www.prageru.com/dennis-pragers-letter-to-candace-owens.
44. https://amgreatness.com/2019/11/21/clearing-the-air-on-the-right.
45. https://x.com/charliekirk11/status/1519720775871127552?lang=en.
46. Ali Breland, "Charlie Kirk Doesn't Really Seem to Mind White Nationalism," *Mother Jones*, February 13, 2024, https://www.motherjones.com/politics/2024/02/charlie-kirk-whiteness-turning-points-usa.
47. "The Great Replacement Theory Isn't Theory, It's Reality," *The Charlie Kirk Show*, April 30, 2024, https://thecharliekirkshow.com/podcasts/the-charlie-kirk-show/the-great-replacement-isnt-theory-its-reality.
48. Thomas Beaumont, "Charlie Kirk Exploits Racial Divide to Reach Gen Z," Associated Press, November 18, 2021, https://apnews.com/article/charlie-kirk-right-wing-provocateur-gen-z-race-5b57b4178fec39f30f3caad77b93c087.
49. Allan Smith, Henry J. Gomez, Matt Dixon, and Vaughn Hillyard, "Conservative Activist Charlie Kirk Helped Oust Ronna McDaniel at the RNC. Now the Knives Are out for Him," NBC News, February 18, 2024, https://www.nbcnews.com/politics/donald-trump/charlie-kirk-ronna-mcdaniel-rnc-trump-rcna139288.

Chapter 6: What's Really Happening

1. "Jack Van Impe—Book of Daniel Unsealed," August 2, 2013, https://www.youtube.com/watch?v=LrzsbiVelMo.
2. Andrew Gardner, "Why Are Christians So Susceptible to Conspiracy?" *Baptist News Global*, August 31, 2020, https://baptistnews.com/article/why-are-christians-so-susceptible-to-conspiracy.

3. Jack Van Impe, *Revelation Revealed* (Thomas Nelson, 1997), 204.
4. Richard Hofstadter, *"The Paranoid Style in American Politics" and Other Essays* (Vintage Books, 1965), xxvi.
5. Daniel Cox, "Rise of Conspiracies Reveals an Evangelical Divide in the GOP," Survey Center on American Life, February 12, 2021, https://www.americansurveycenter.org/rise-of-conspiracies-reveal-an-evangelical-divide-in-the-gop.
6. "Happening Now with Charlie Kirk and Jack Hibbs," February 4, 2023, https://www.youtube.com/watch?v=7bQofg8a9bU.
7. "You're Entering the Final Phase before Victory," Human Events, August 10, 2022, https://humanevents.com/2022/08/10/charlie-kirk-youre-entering-the-final-phase-before-victory.
8. Johnny Enlow, *The Seven Mountain Mantle* (Creation House, 2009), 86.
9. "An Interview with Charlie Kirk; Understanding the Times and the Role of Believers," Awaken Church, March 31, 2023, https://www.youtube.com/watch?v=cJsIwBEVAM4.
10. Ben Stein, "The War to Clean Up TV," *Saturday Review*, February 1981, published as appendix 4 in *Bad News for Modern Man*, by Franky Schaeffer (Crossway Books, 1984), 161.
11. Mark Ward Sr., "'From a Christian Perspective': News/Talk in Evangelical Mass Media," in *News on the Right: Studying Conservative News Cultures*, ed. Andrew Joseph Bauer and Anthony M. Nadler (Oxford University Press, 2020), 18.
12. Pat Robertson, "A Christian Action Plan for the 1980s," *Biblical Economics Today* 2, no. 6 (December/January 1980), C-16.
13. Francis Schaeffer, *How Should We Then Live?* (Crossway Books, 1976), 240.
14. "How Should We Then Live, Episode 10: Final Choices," https://www.youtube.com/watch?v=o6TG_K39KoU.
15. Quoted in Paul F. Parsons, *Inside America's Christian Schools* (Mercer University Press, 1988), 20.
16. Charles Krauthammer, "The Humanist Phantom," *New Republic*, July 21, 1981, 22.
17. Tim LaHaye, *The Battle for the Mind* (Fleming Revell, 1980), 9–10.
18. Tim Dickinson, "Charlie Kirk's 'Turning Point' Pivots to Christian Nationalism," *Rolling Stone*, May 23, 2023, https://www.rollingstone.com/politics/politics-features/charlie-kirk-turning-point-usa-pivots-to-christian-nationalism-1234740083.
19. Allan Smith, Henry J. Gomez, Matt Dixon, and Vaughn Hillyard, "Conservative Activist Charlie Kirk Helped Oust Ronna McDaniel at the RNC. Now the Knives Are out for Him," NBC News, February 18, 2024, https://www.nbcnews.com/politics/donald-trump/charlie-kirk-ronna-mcdaniel-rnc-trump-rcna139288.

20. "Liberal Bias Starts in High School Economics Textbooks," April 26, 2012, https://www.breitbart.com/politics/2012/04/26/liberal-bias-starts-in-high-school-economics.
21. "Charlie Kirk—The Conservative Forum," September 10, 2015, https://www.youtube.com/watch?v=ihaMOHCVYsQ&t=164s.
22. https://www.tpusa.com/publications.
23. Charlie Kirk, "Obama's Silent Regulatory Army Is Still on the March," *The Hill*, May 5, 2018, https://thehill.com/opinion/campaign/386387-obamas-silent-regulatory-army-marches-on.
24. https://mediabiasfactcheck.com/turning-point-usa; https://adfontesmedia.com/turning-point-usa-bias-and-reliability; https://adfontesmedia.com/charlie-kirk-show-bias-and-reliability; https://www.politifact.com/personalities/charlie-kirk.
25. "Charlie Kirk to NRB: Church Is the Last Firewall for Freedom," April 5, 2022, https://nrb.org/charlie-kirk-to-nrb-church-is-the-last-firewall-for-freedom.
26. "Charlie Kirk—The Great Reset and the Coming New World Order," *Real Life with Jack Hibbs*, September 30, 2022, https://www.youtube.com/watch?v=gkBbMokaxmE.
27. "Will the Future Be Human?" January 31, 2018, https://www.youtube.com/watch?v=npfShBTNp3Q.
28. "Attention, World Citizens—The Role of God Will Now Be Played by the Men in Davos," Human Events, January 20, 2023, https://humanevents.com/2023/01/20/kirk-attention-world-citizens-the-role-of-god-will-now-be-played-by-the-men-in-davos.
29. "Yuval Noah Harari in Conversation with Sara Pascoe," November 26, 2020, https://youtu.be/18Oyqn6ahGg?si=SOwlMFOQRBzY5wEF; "Read Yuval Harari's Blistering Warning to Davos in Full," World Economic Forum, January 24, 2020, https://www.weforum.org/agenda/2020/01/yuval-hararis-warning-davos-speech-future-predications.
30. David Klepper, "Grave Peril of Digital Conspiracy Theories: 'What Happens When No One Believes Anything Anymore?'" January 31, 2024, https://apnews.com/article/dangers-of-digital-conspiracy-theories-ec21024be1ed377a35fb235d9fa2af36.
31. "An Interview with Charlie Kirk—Understanding the Times and the Role of Believers," Awaken Church, March 31, 2023, https://www.youtube.com/watch?v=cJsIwBEVAM4.

Chapter 7: The Left Can't Meme

1. Francis Schaeffer, *Art and the Bible* (Hodder and Stoughton, 1973), 58.
2. Andy Crouch, "Being Culture Makers," January 2007, https://andy-crouch.com/articles/being_culture_makers.

3. Byron York, "In Politics Fight, Breitbart Knew Culture Is Key," *Washington Examiner*, March 1, 2012, https://www.washingtonexaminer.com/news/1316438/in-politics-fight-breitbart-knew-culture-is-key.
4. Stephanie Condon, "Breitbart: Conservatives to Go 'On Offense' against Media, Professors," CBS News, February 20, 2010, https://www.cbsnews.com/news/breitbart-conservatives-to-go-on-offense-against-media-professors; Lawrence Meyers, "Politics Really Is Downstream from Culture," Breitbart, August 21, 2011, https://www.breitbart.com/entertainment/2011/08/22/politics-really-is-downstream-from-culture.
5. Bill Bright and Ron Jenson, *Kingdoms at War: Tactics for Victory in Nine Spiritual War Zones* (Here's Life, 1986), 168; Loren Cunningham, *Making Jesus Lord* (YWAM Publishing, 1988), 140.
6. https://www.tpusa.com/breakaway.
7. https://www.jonrootlive.com/about-1.
8. "Breakaway with Jon Root Starting September 14," September 9, 2021, https://www.youtube.com/watch?v=CKbGeliNICM.
9. https://www.youtube.com/watch?v=ZatGmCnAz0U&t=11s.
10. "Why America Should Look Like Sports with Charlie Kirk," December 7, 2021, https://www.youtube.com/watch?v=QlTTTSHiIPs.
11. https://www.tpusa.com/poplitics.
12. "Spoopy Hollywood Stars & Rapper YG Throws a Trump Tantrum," October 28, 2019, https://www.youtube.com/watch?v=Mwg_Z_ipthE&list=PLnZT7Gz_VSN5GEpdUo87cscOAK-b53TOM&index=87.
13. Alex Nichols, "The Right's Attempt at Pop Culture Is Hilariously Wrong," *The Outline*, December 12, 2019, https://theoutline.com/post/8418/poplitics-the-patriot-awards-republican-pop-culture-is-horrible.
14. "The Role Your Church Should Play in Addressing Political and Cultural Issues," September 23, 2022, https://www.youtube.com/watch?v=Ms8tQNaeBoU.
15. "Conservative Taylor Swift Hate Is Pushing Me Away," January 31, 2024, https://www.youtube.com/watch?v=xZbghUmJifo.
16. Tess Owen, "They Love Jesus, Bon Iver, and Incels: Inside America's New Ultranationalist Youth Movement," Vice, June 7, 2022, https://www.vice.com/en/article/groyper-young-christian-nationalists-movement.
17. "White Boy Summer: From Meme to Mobilization," Anti-Defamation League, June 29, 2021, https://www.adl.org/resources/blog/white-boy-summer-meme-mobilization; "How White Boy Summer Turned into a Transnational Hate Campaign," Global Project Against Hate and Extremism, July 2, 2024, https://globalextremism.org/post/wbs.
18. "Goodbye Spillover," August 1, 2024, https://youtu.be/zs9X_pZkaTU?si=BzGSM_Oy6Dumvzhl.
19. https://www.youtube.com/playlist?list=PLxx4kcMvHrwIFMnpmdY0_KgH93XIWsQ6j.

20. Tom Gerken, "Is This 1921 Cartoon the First Ever Meme?" April 16, 2018, https://www.bbc.com/news/blogs-trending-43783521.
21. Lennlee Keep, "From Kilroy to Pepe: A Brief History of Memes," PBS, October 9, 2020, https://www.pbs.org/independentlens/blog/from-kilroy-to-pepe-a-brief-history-of-memes.
22. Bradley Wiggins, *The Discursive Power of Memes in Digital Culture: Ideology, Semiotics, and Intertextuality* (Taylor & Francis, 2019), 1.
23. Matthew Taylor, *The Violent Take It by Force* (Broadleaf Books, 2024), 152.
24. 2017–18 Turning Point chapter handbook, https://web.archive.org/web/20180227185002/https://tpusa.com/wp-content/uploads/2017/06/ChapterHandbook_CE2017-2018_FINAL.pdf.
25. "'Affirmative Action' Bake-Sale Stirs Up Controversy," Associated Press, September 22, 2017, https://www.koat.com/article/affirmative-action-bake-sale-stirs-up-controversy/12455319.
26. https://www.tpusa.com/chapterhandbook.
27. Isaac Stanley-Becker, "Pro-Trump Youth Group Enlists Teens in Secretive Campaign Likened to a 'Troll Farm,' Prompting Rebuke by Facebook and Twitter," *Washington Post*, September 15, 2020, https://www.washingtonpost.com/politics/turning-point-teens-disinformation-trump/2020/09/15/c84091ae-f20a-11ea-b796-2dd09962649c_story.html.
28. Josh Fiallo, "Right-Wing Influencer Accused of Taking Kremlin Cash Fired," *Daily Beast*, September 5, 2024, https://www.thedailybeast.com/lauren-chen-fired-blaze-media-axes-creator-caught-up-in-russian-influence-scandal.
29. Kyle Mantyla, "Benny Johnson Spreads False Christian Nationalist History," Right Wing Watch, April 4, 2024, https://www.rightwingwatch.org/post/benny-johnson-spreads-false-christian-nationalist-history.
30. Ben Terris, "Benny Johnson Got Fired at BuzzFeed. You Will Believe What Happened Next," *Washington Post*, June 9, 2015, https://www.washingtonpost.com/lifestyle/style/benny-johnson-got-fired-at-buzzfeed-you-will-believe-what-happened-next/2015/06/09/da9fe3f8-e37f-11e4-b510-962fcfabc310_story.html.
31. Brittany Shepherd, "The Mission: Make Conservatism Cool. The Strategy: A Mechanical Bull and a Cardboard Cutout of AOC," *Washingtonian*, March 1, 2019, https://www.washingtonian.com/2019/03/01/the-mission-make-conservatism-cool-the-strategy-a-mechanical-bull-and-a-cardboard-cutout-of-aoc.
32. Ben Smith, *Traffic: Genius, Rivalry, and Delusion in the Billion-Dollar Race to Go Viral* (Penguin, 2024), 185–94.
33. "Social Media Sensation Benny Johnson Stars on NewsMax TV," NewsMax, September 24, 2020, https://www.newsmax.com/newsfront/benny-johnson-newsmaxtv-debut-the-benny-report/2020/09/24/id/988634.
34. Andrew Kirell, "Serial Plagiarist Benny Johnson Joining Charlie Kirk's Turning Point USA," *Daily Beast*, February 6, 2019, https://www

.thedailybeast.com/serial-plagiarist-benny-johnson-joining-charlie-kirks-turning-point-usa.
35. Charlie Kirk, *Time for a Turning Point: Setting a Course toward Free Markets and Limited Government for Future Generations* (Post Hill Press, 2016), 13.
36. Alex Bruesewitz, *Winning the Social Media War: How Conservatives Can Fight Back, Reclaim the Narrative, and Turn the Tides against the Left* (Bombardier Books, 2022), iv.
37. Jessica Klein, "In America's Meme War, the Left and Right Are Fighting Different Battles," *Daily Dot*, July 23, 2019, https://www.dailydot.com/unclick/meme-warfare-left-right/
38. Aaron Blake, "Nikki Haley Warns against 'Owning the Libs.' That's Basically Trump's Entire Political Strategy," *Washington Post*, July 24, 2018, https://www.washingtonpost.com/news/the-fix/wp/2018/07/24/nikki-haley-warns-against-owning-the-libs-thats-basically-trumps-entire-political-strategy.
39. Adam Rubenstein, "Kid Trump," *Washington Examiner*, August 2, 2018, https://www.washingtonexaminer.com/politics/1463441/kid-trump.
40. "Political History of Internet Culture," Creatorpedia, https://creatorpedia.fandom.com/wiki/Political_history_of_internet_culture.
41. Sean Illing, "Why Conservatives Are Winning the Internet," *Vox*, June 3, 2019, https://www.vox.com/policy-and-politics/2019/6/3/18624687/conservatism-liberals-internet-activism-jen-schradie.
42. Stephanie Mencimer, "'The Left Can't Meme': How Right-Wing Groups Are Training the Next Generation of Social Media Warriors," *Mother Jones*, April 2, 2019, https://www.motherjones.com/politics/2019/04/right-wing-groups-are-training-young-conservatives-to-win-the-next-meme-war.
43. Turning Point USA, September 19, 2022, https://fb.watch/uxpoVtUsuZ.
44. Matt Masters, "Turning Point USA Event Coaches Students on Fighting the 'Culture War' with Memes and Ridicule," October 1, 2022, https://www.thenewstn.com/schools/turning-point-usa-event-coaches-students-on-fighting-the-culture-war-with-memes-and-ridicule/article_90e02fc2-40ea-11ed-873f-9bd74e3353aa.html.
45. "Benny Johnson's The Left Can't Meme," January 15, 2023, https://archive.org/details/the-left-cant-meme/The+Left+Can%E2%80%99t+Meme+S01E01%3A+Elon+Derangement+Syndrome.mp4.
46. "The Left Can't Meme with Benny Johnson Exclusively on Parler," July 29, 2022, https://www.youtube.com/watch?v=S2JchYlRnJ8.
47. Makena Kelly, "Parler's New Owners Swear This Time Will Be Different," *Wired*, March 28, 2024, https://www.wired.com/story/parler-app-store-free-speech-censorship.
48. Jonathan Chait, "How J. D. Vance and the Online Right Sabotaged Trump at the Debate," September 11, 2024, https://nymag.com/intelligencer/article/trump-debate-eating-pets-j-d-vance-cats-dogs-springfield.html.

49. Emily Shugerman, "Turning Point USA: How One Student in a Diaper Caused an Eruption in the Conservative Youth Organization," *The Independent*, February 26, 2018, https://www.independent.co.uk/news/world/americas/diaper-turning-point-usa-kent-state-student-conservative-youth-repulican-kaitlin-bennett-a8230021.html.
50. Alex Kuang, "Kent State Students Dress Up as Babies, Claiming That 'Safe Spaces Are for Children,'" *Daily Pennsylvanian*, October 25, 2017, https://www.thedp.com/article/2017/10/kent-state-students-dress-up-as-babies-claiming-that-safe-spaces-are-for-children.
51. Michael Vasquez, "Leaked Memo from Conservative Group Cautions Students to Stay Away from Turning Point USA," *Chronicle of Higher Education*, June 15, 2018, https://www.chronicle.com/article/leaked-memo-from-conservative-group-cautions-students-to-stay-away-from-turning-point-usa.
52. Neil Postman, *Amusing Ourselves to Death* (Penguin, 2006), 3.

Afterword

1. "A Call to Defend Democracy and Pluralism," *Eyes Right!* ed. Chip Berlet (South End Press, 1995), 317–26.
2. Bruce Barron, *Heaven on Earth: The Social and Political Agendas of Dominion Theology* (Zondervan, 1992), 166–69.

Index

Adams, John, 70
affirmative action bake sale, 136
Ahn, Ché, 65, 70–71
AIDS/HIV, 82
Alfred the Great (king), 49
American history, in education, 29, 38, 63–64
American Renewal Project, 56
Amusing Ourselves to Death (Postman), 143
antidemocracy, 50–51, 53–54, 68–70, 74
anti-Semitism, 72–73, 109
apocalypse. *See* eschatology
apostles, 16, 64–66, 103–4
Arizona, education in, 28, 36–37, 40
Arnn, Larry, 30–31
Art and the Bible (Schaeffer), 127
athletes, 92–93, 129–31

Babylon, 32, 34, 55
bake sales, 136
Barron, Bruce, 57, 146
Barton, David, 37, 64, 67
Bible
    Babylonian education in, 32, 34
    on church and state separation, 33–35
    on civic action, 68
    on cultural war, justification for, 62
    on dominionism, 15
    on economy, 99–100, 104–5
    on *ekklesia*, 71
    on evangelicalism, 8
    on homosexuality, 80
    on Jesus' return, 113–14
    on marriage, 89
    on nations, blessed vs. cursed, 68
    on news, 115
    on new world order, 124
    seven, the number in, 13, 115
    on wealth transfer, 102–3
    on women, 89–90
biblical-based educational curriculum, 38–39
biblical citizenship, 67–68
biblical movement, of government, 44–46. *See also* government, mountain of
biblical worldview, 60–63
Black prosperity, 106–9
Blexit, 107–8
Bonhoeffer, Dietrich, 34–35, 65
book bans, 39
Bowler, Kate, 106

Breakaway, 130
Breitbart, Andrew, 128–29
Breitbart media, 5, 28, 121, 128–29
Bright, Bill
   on biblical citizenship, 67
   on biblical government, 46
   Cunningham meeting with, 1–2, 14
   on education, 26–27, 41
   on entertainment, 128–29
   on gender roles, 88
   political agenda of, 9–10
   Schaeffer's impact on, 11
   seven mountains mandate movement and, 7–10
Bright, Vonette, 88–89
business, mountain of, 97–112
   capitalism and, 99–103, 110, 112, 121–22
   dominionism through, 104–6 (*see also* dominionism, Christian)
   great transfer of wealth and, 98–102, 109–11
   prophecies of wealth and, 101–4
   racial divides and, 109–11
   victim mentality and, 106–9
Buzzfeed, 138

California, politics in, 54, 56
Cameron, Paul, 81
campaign, Trump. *See* Trump, Donald
Campbell, Caleb, 74
Campus Crusade for Christ, 8, 41, 88
capitalism, 99–103, 110, 112, 121–22. *See also* free markets
Capitol insurrection, 2–4, 51, 59–60, 65, 135, 141
Capps, Charles, 101–2
Case for Christian Nationalism, The (Wolfe), 51, 58
charismatic movement, 15–16, 65
Charlie Kirk Show, The
   about, 5
   credibility of, 123
   Driscoll on, 94
   Greene on, 44
   on masculinity, 86
   McCoy on, 55
   popularity of, 121
   on predator catching incident, 78–79
charter schools, 29, 36–37. *See also* private schools
Chen, Lauren, 96, 137
Christendom, 49–50
Christian Heritage Academy (IL), 31–32
Christianization of America, early thought on, 13–15. *See also* individual mountains
Christian Manifesto, The (Schaeffer), 12, 50
Christian nationalism
   about, 4
   American origin, thought on, 132, 137
   antidemocratic agenda of, 50–53, 74
   communities of, 49–50
   democracy ignored by, 47
   economic theology of, 100
   education and, 24, 26, 36–37, 41–42
   eschatology beliefs of, 26, 73
   Greene and, 43 (*see also* Greene, Marjorie Taylor)
   insurrection and (*see* Capitol insurrection)
   Kirk and, 94, 100
   LGBTQ and, 79–80
   promotion event for, 68
   rejection of, by Evangelical Free Church of America (EFCA), 39
   response to, 145–46
   Trump and, 50–51, 65, 70
   violence and, 3–4, 50–53
   Wallnau and, 17 (*see also* Wallnau, Lance)
   See also individual mountains

Index   175

church
    citizen training within, 66–68
    failure of, 61–62
    growth movement, Wagner's, 14
    as legislative body of kingdom of God, 70–72
    as nation's sovereignty, 55
    Satan in, 60
    and state separation, 17–18, 33–35, 54
cities, conservative indoctrination of, 47–50, 104
citizenship, biblical, 67–68
City Elders, 50, 53
civic action, call for, 68–72
civic training, 67
civil rights, 29–30, 97. *See also* racism
Clark, Alex, 131–33
Clarkston, Frederick, 50, 56
classical education model, 37
clergy. *See* pastors
colleges. *See* higher education
comics, as memes, 135
common grace, 15
common morality, 30
communities, Christian, 47–50, 104
complementarianism, 90–91, 93, 95
compound raids, 52–53
Conservative Baptist Network, 66–67
conservative media outlets, 118
conspiracy theories, media and
    democracy and, impact on, 125–26
    eschatology and, 114–17
    Kirk on, 121–22
    mindset of, 115–16
    promotion strategy of, 122–25
    as secular propaganda, 115, 118–20
COVID-19 pandemic, 23, 55, 63, 123–25
cowardice, 64
Crouch, Andy, 127–28
cryptocurrency, 99

Cuba conspiracy theory, 123
cultural mandate, 14–16, 47, 61, 65. *See also* dominionism, Christian
cultural spheres, 13–14, 25, 46, 61. *See also* list, of cultural domains
Culture Making (Crouch), 127
culture war, 61–62, 127–28, 133–34, 139–41. *See also* entertainment, mountain of
Cunningham, Loren
    on biblical government, 46
    Black prosperity and, 106–9
    Bright, meeting with, 1–2, 14
    on entertainment, 129
    on gender roles, 89
    Schaeffer's impact on, 11
    seven mountain movement mandate origin and, 8–10
    See also mind molders
curriculum, educational, 29–32, 37–39

D'Almeida, Kalen, 77–79
Daniel (biblical figure), as public education metaphor, 34
Davis, Stephen, 106–7
Dawkins, Richard, 134
Dawson, John, 48
deep state, 116, 122
democracy
    capitalism's impact on, 112
    conservative family values and, 95–96
    conspiracy theories' impact on, 125–26
    destruction of, 44–45
    education's importance in, 42
    entertainment's impact on, 143
    ignored, by Christian leaders, 46–47
    violence against, 3–4, 50–53
    (*see also* Capitol insurrection)
    "we the people," Kirk's use of, 55

Democratic Party/liberalist left
  Black exodus from, 107–8
  Clark on, 132
  economy and, 97
  national divorce and, 43
  social media and, 140–41
  voting rights of, in red states, 44–45
  See also liberal indoctrination, claims of
demons/demonic activity, 15, 27, 44, 48. *See also* Satan
desegregation, school, 24–25
DeYoung, Kevin, 95
Diamond, Sara, 25–26
diaper event, 141–42
dispensationalism, 72, 114–15, 117
divorce, national, 43–44
dominionism, Christian, 13, 15, 17, 54–56, 62, 104–6, 146. *See also* cultural mandate
Drag Queen Story Hour, 40
Draper, Jimmy, 12
drift, secular, 12
Driscoll, Mark, 94–95, 131
Du Mez, Kristen Kobes, 83

Eastman, John, 31
economy, 39, 73, 123–24. *See also* business, mountain of; capitalism; free markets
education, mountain of, 21–42
  of American history, 29, 38, 63–64
  charter schools, 29, 36–37
  conservative indoctrination of, 29–32
  curriculum, 29–32, 37–39
  in democracies, importance of, 42
  eschatological beliefs and, 25–26
  higher, 6, 21–23, 29–31, 39–41
  homeschooling, 25, 38
  Kirk's hostility toward, 22–24
  liberal indoctrination in, 21–23, 27–34, 40–41, 121–22

  private, 24–25, 29, 33
  public, call to remove students from, 33–34
  public, Christianity silencing of, 32
  public, history of, 26–27
  punishment of, 24
  reconstructionism and, 24–25
  vouchers' impact on, 35–37
  watchlists of, 21–22, 35
ekklesia, 70–72
elders, 50
Eldredge, John, 84–85
end-times, 25–26, 51, 72–73, 114–17
Enlow, Johnny, 27, 41, 62, 117
entertainment, mountain of, 127–43
  Christian vs. secular, 127–29
  democracy and, impact on, 143
  memes and (*see* memes)
  pop culture and, 131–34
  sports and, 129–31
enthymemes, 135
entrepreneurship, 103, 105
eschatology, 25–26, 51, 72–73, 114–17
Ethridge, Tyler, 59–60
Evangelical Free Church of America (EFCA), 39

Falwell, Jerry, 11, 41, 118
Falwell, Jerry Jr., 42
family, mountain of
  democracy and, impact on, 95–96
  gender roles in (*see* gender roles)
  LGBTQ matters and (*see* LGBTQ matters)
  marriage model for, 89–93
  masculinity and, 82–85
  mentorships for, 94–95
  predator catching incident and, 77–79
Feminine Mystique, The (Friedan), 82
feminism, 9, 82–83, 87. *See also* women
firearms, 21, 140
5Cs schools, 37

Fox News, 118
Franklin, Jentzen, 131
free markets, 17, 101–2, 105–7, 123. *See also* capitalism
Friedan, Betty, 80, 88
Friess, Foster, 18, 151n44
Fronczak, Joseph, 69
Frontlines (Turning Point investigation team), 77–79, 122–23
fundamentalism, Christian, 7, 26, 40–42, 127

gay marriage, 81–82. *See also* LGBTQ matters
gender roles
   evangelical thought on, 82–85
   LGBTQ matters and, 80–82
   of men, 80, 85–87
   pop culture and, 133–34
   of women, 80–82, 87–89, 133
God
   church as legislative body of, 70–72
   conspiracies against, 115–17 (*see also* conspiracy theories, media and)
   on economy, 97–98
   government and, 67, 92
   schools turning students against (*see* liberal indoctrination, claims of)
   Trump as chosen by, 54–55
   on tyranny for liberty, 52
   visions from, 1–2
   wealth and, 98–99, 101–4, 106 (*see also* business, mountain of)
government, mountain of, 43–58
   antidemocracy, states and, 53–54
   biblical movement of, 44–45
   church power over, 6
   church separation and, 17–18, 33–35, 54
   democracy ignored in, 46–47
   dominion of, 54–56
   downsizing of, 43–44
   regulations of, 97, 99
   seven mountain movement mandate leaders on, 46
   spiritual mapping and, 47–50
   tyranny and, 50–53
Graham, Billy, 47
Great Evangelical Disaster, The (Schaeffer), 12
great replacement theory, 111, 122–23
Great Reset conspiracy theory, 123–25
great transfer of wealth, 98–102, 109–11
Green, Rick, 67
Greene, Marjorie Taylor, 43–45
grifting, 101
Grudem, Wayne, 31–32
gun laws, 21, 140

Haggard, Ted, 49
Hamon, Bill, 104, 106
Hannah-Jones, Nikole, 30
Harari, Yuval Noah, 124
Henry, Carl, 61
Hertzberg, Hutz, 31
Hibbs, Jack, 68, 123
higher education, 6, 21–23, 29–31, 39–41
Hillsdale College (MI), 29
HIV/AIDS, 82
Hofstadter, Richard, 116
homeschooling, 25, 38
homosexuality. *See* LGBTQ matters
Hood, Greg, 71
Horowitz, David, 22, 107
How Should We Then Live? (Schaeffer), 11–12, 119
How the Right Lost Its Mind (Sykes), 101
humanism, secular, 9, 26–27, 119–20

immigration/immigrants, 110–11, 122–23, 141
indoctrination, conservative. *See individual mountains*

indoctrination, liberal. *See* liberal indoctrination, claims of
Ingersoll, Julie, 24–25
Institutes of Biblical Law, The (Rushdoony), 13
insurrection, Capitol. *See* Capitol insurrection
internet activism, 140. *See also* memes
Islam, 73–74
Israel, 72–73
Ivy League schools, 41

January 6, 2021. *See* Capitol insurrection
Jesus and John Wayne (Du Mez), 83
Johnson, Benny, 132, 134, 137–41
Johnson, Mike, 45
Judaism, 72–73, 109
Judeo-Christian, phrase of, 73

Kassian, Mary, 90
Kennedy, D. James, 61
Kent State University (OH), 142
kingdom of God, 70–72
Kingdoms at War: Tactics for Victory in Nine Spiritual War Zones (Bright), 10, 26, 128–29
Kirk, Charlie
  about, 5–6
  on antidemocracy, 68–70
  on apostles, 66
  Arnn and, 31
  on biblical citizenship, 66
  on biblical worldview crisis, 62–63
  church and state separation and, 17–18
  conspiracy theories and, 116–17, 121–25
  on COVID-19, 55, 63
  CPAC speech by (2020), 6, 17–18
  education and, 22–24, 28–29, 40, 121–22 (*see also* Turning Point Academy)
  on government, 44
  on Greene, 45
  hostility of, 22–24, 28–29
  ideological shifts of, 56–57
  Lane and, 56
  on LGTBQ matters, 80–82
  list of cultural domains and, 4–7, 17–18
  marriage of, 90–93
  McCoy and, 55
  meme of, 141–42
  mentors of, 94–95
  racism of, 109–11
  radio show of (*see Charlie Kirk Show, The*)
  on religious freedom, 73–74
  on sports, 130–31
  Trump and, 5, 17–19, 52, 69, 98, 111, 122
  Trump Jr. and, 19
  wealth creation of, 100–101
  See also Turning Point *headings*
Kirk, Erika, 88–93, 95–96
Knowles, Michael, 79
Kuyper, Abraham, 14–15, 25, 60–61

L'Abri, 11
LaHaye, Tim, 26, 120
Lane, David, 56
law, God's, 14–15, 31, 46, 54, 72, 80, 104
leadership, Christian, Schaeffer's impact on, 11
Leadership Congress, 67–68
Left Behind, 26
legislative training, 67
LGBTQ matters
  advocacy, 40
  family and, 79–80
  marriage, 81–82
  transgender identity, 40, 77–81, 92–93
  Turning Point on, 79–80

liberal indoctrination, claims of
    in education, 21–23, 27–34, 40–41, 121–22
    on masculinity, 85
    by media, 116–17
    in sports, 130
Liberty Baptist College (VA), 41–42
Libs of TikTok, 87
Lindsey, Hal, 72
line of despair, 12
list, of cultural domains
    of Bright and Cunningham, 1–4, 149n2
    Cunningham's use of, 9
    Kirk and, 4–7, 17–18
    as mandate, 14–16
    mountain metaphor and, 16–17
    pre-1975, 7, 13–14
    Schaeffer and, 10–12

MacDonald, James, 94
man and machine, merging of
    conspiracy theory, 123–24
mandate, cultural. *See* cultural mandate
Mann, Horace, 27
mapping, spiritual, 15, 47–50
marketplace apostle, 103–4
marriage
    gay, 81–82
    gender roles and, 80–82, 85–89
    model for conservative, 89–93
    See also family, mountain of
Martin, Stephen, 33–34
Marty, Martin, 119–20
masculinity, 80, 83–87
mask policies, COVID, 23
McCartney, Bill, 83
McCoy, Rob, 18, 54–55, 94, 110
McDaniel, Ronna, 19
media, mountain of, 97–126
    Bible and, 115
    conservative outlets of, 118
    conspiracy theories and (*See* conspiracy theories, media and)
    liberal indoctrination and, 116–17
    redemptive, 117
memes
    about, 134–35
    B. Johnson and, 137–41
    culture war and, 139–41
    diaper event and, 141–42
    Turning Point's use of, 136–37, 139
men, 80, 85–87, 133–34
Metaxas, Eric, 69
Middle Eastern conflicts, 113
Miller, Steven Patrick, 7
mind molders, 9, 62, 105, 119. *See also* Cunningham, Loren
ministers. *See* pastors
minority rule, 46–47
mocking, through memes, 140–41
money. *See* business, mountain of
motherhood, 88. *See also under* gender roles: of women
mountain metaphor, about, 16–17, 105
movies, 128
Mozingo, Spencer, 86

National Day of Prayer, 66
national divorce, 43–44
nationalism, Christian. *See* Christian nationalism
Nazi regime, 34–35, 65, 109
New Apostolic Reformation, 16, 65
news. *See* media, mountain of
new world order, 102, 114, 124
New World Order, The (Robertson), 102
1960s, 7
North, Gary, 16, 46–47

Ohio, Haitian immigrants in, 141
Oklahoma Department of Education, 37
One Nation under God (Walton), 14–15
Owens, Candace, 107–9

"own the libs" meme, 139

Paine, Thomas, 69
pandemic, COVID-19, 23, 55, 63, 123–25
paranoia mindset, 115–16
"Paranoid Style in American Politics, The" (Hofstadter), 116
pardons, Capitol insurrection and, 4, 59
Parler show (B. Johnson's), 139–40
participatory antidemocracy, 69
pastors, 33–35, 59–60, 62–64
patriarchy. *See* gender roles; masculinity
Patriot Academy, 67
Peacocke, Dennis, 104
pedophile raid, 77–79
persons of color, prosperity of, 106–9
philanthropy, 98
pluralism, democracy, defense of, 145–46
pluralism, religious, 57, 72–74
politics
    entertainment and, 128–29
    masculinity and, 86–87
    memes and, 136–37 (*see also* memes)
    pop culture and, 131–34
    sports and, 129–31
    See also government, mountain of; Trump, Donald
Pollution and the Death of Man (Schaeffer), 14
pop culture, 131–34
POPlitics radio show, 131–33
Posobiec, Jack, 122, 133
Postman, Neil, 143
postmillennialism, 26
poverty, 103–4, 106–9
Prager, Dennis, 37, 73
prayer
    National Day of, 66
    spiritual mapping and, 48–49
predator catching incident, of Turning Point, 77–79

premillennialism, 26, 115
private schools, 24–25, 29, 33. *See also* charter schools
privilege, Christian, 4, 6, 60
professors, 21–22, 39–41. *See also* higher education
Professors, The: The 101 Most Dangerous Academics in America (Horowitz), 22
Promise Keepers, 83
propaganda, secular news as, 115, 118–20
prophecies/prophets, 98–99, 101–5, 114, 117. *See also* apostles
prophetic memes, 135
Prophets and Personal Prophecy (Hamon), 104
prosperity gospel, 101–4, 108
Protestantism, 16, 57, 74
pro-White markets, 109–11. *See also* racism

racism
    in business, 109–11
    education and, 24–25, 30
    government downsizing and, 44
    memes and, 132–33
    victim mentality and, 106–9
radio, 118, 131–33. *See also Charlie Kirk Show, The*; media, mountain of
Raichik, Chaya, 87–88
rapture, 25–26, 51, 72–73, 114–17
reconstructionism, Christian, 13–14, 24–25, 46
Reformed movement, 16
religion, mountain of, 59–75
    antidemocracy in, 68–70
    apostolic empowerment and, 64–66
    biblical worldview and, 60–61
    evangelical institutional empowerment, 66–68
    legislative body of, church as, 70–72
    pastoral empowerment and, 62–64
    religious freedom and, 72–75

spiritual warfare in, 61–62
state separation and, 17–18, 33–35, 54
religious freedom, 57, 72–75
religious privilege, 60
religious right, 9
replacement theory (immigration), 111, 122–23
republic, America as, 42, 69–70
Republican Party (GOP)/conservative right
   on City Elders, 50
   on conspiracy theories, 116
   on educational curriculum, 29
   Greene, 43–45
   memes and, 141
   seven mountain movement and, 3
   Turning Point's impact on, 19
   See also individual mountains
ridicule, through memes, 140–41
Robertson, Pat, 97–98, 102, 119
role-interchangeability, 90
Root, Jon, 130–31
Ruby Ridge compound raid, 52–53
Rushdoony, R. J., 13–15, 24–25, 46
Russian interference, in Trump campaign, 137

Satan, 8, 27, 48, 60. *See also* demons/demonic activity
Schaeffer, Francis
   about, 10–12
   on art and Christianity, 127
   on biblical government, 46
   on media, 119
   on spheres, 14
   on tyranny, 50–51
   on worldview, 61
school board watchlist, 35
school choice, 24
schools. *See* education, mountain of
Scofield Reference Bible, 114
Scottsdale (AZ) school district, 23, 28

secular drift, 12
secularism
   drift toward, 12
   in education, 32–33, 41
   in entertainment, 127–28
   founding fathers and, 18, 30
   in government, 47
   in media, 115, 118, 120
   See also humanism, secular; liberal indoctrination, claims of
Seidel, Andrew, 17
Sell, Melissa, 126
seven, prevalence of in Bible, 13, 115
seven mountain movement mandate
   business, 97–112 (*see also* business, mountain of)
   education, mountain of, 21–42 (*see also* education, mountain of)
   entertainment, 127–43 (*see also* entertainment, mountain of)
   family, 77–96 (*see also* family, mountain of)
   government, mountain of, 43–58 (*see also* government, mountain of)
   media, mountain of, 113–26 (*see also* media, mountain of)
   origin of, 1–20 (*see also* list, of cultural domains)
   religion, mountain of, 59–75 (*see also* religion, mountain of)
Seven Mountain Prophecy, The (Enlow), 27
1776 Commission, 30
seven-year tribulation period, 115
1619 Project, 30
Smith, Rob, 80, 107
Social Gospel movement, 26
socialism, 98–99, 101, 112, 136
social media, 19, 136–39. *See also* memes
societal domains. *See* list, of cultural domains
society, infiltration of, 60–61
Soros, George, 98–99

Southern Baptist Convention, 3, 66
speech, freedom of, 142
sphere law, 46
spheres, cultural. *See* cultural spheres
spirit of poverty, 106
spiritual mapping, 15, 47–50
spiritual paranoia, 115
spiritual warfare, 8, 10, 15, 44–45, 47–48, 51–52, 61–62
Spiritual Warfare (Diamond), 25
sports, 92–93, 129–31
state power, 44
states, antidemocracy and, 53–54
Stitt, Kevin (R-Ok), 50
submissiveness, in marriage, 82, 89–90
Summit, The, 85–87
Swift, Taylor, 132
Sykes, Charlie, 101
Sypher, Andrew, 53–54

Taking Our Cities for God (Dawson), 48
Taylor, Matthew, 52, 64, 72, 74, 135
teachers, 21–22, 27, 35, 39–41
television, 118. *See also* media, mountain of
Tender Warriors: God's Intention for a Man (Weber), 83
territorial spirits, 15
Time for a Turning Point (Kirk), 18
toxic masculinity, 85–86. *See also* masculinity
trad wives, 91
transformational coaching, of business leaders, 105
transgender identity, 77–81, 92–93. *See also* LGBTQ matters
Trump, Donald
    Capitol insurrection and, 2–4, 51, 59–60, 65, 141
    Christian nationalists' expectations of, 50–51, 65, 70
    conspiracy theories and, 116, 122
    elections of, 65, 69
    as God picked, 54–55
    Kirk and, 5, 17–19, 52, 69, 98, 111, 122
    memes and, 136, 139, 141
    Russian interference in campaign of, 137
    spirituality of, 51–52
    Turning Point and, 52, 111
    Wallnau on, 17
Trump, Donald Jr., 19
Turner, John G., 10
Turning Point
    antidemocratic movement and, 52–54
    on biblical citizenship, 67–68
    conspiracy theories and, 121–25
    diaper event of, 141–42
    on education (*see* education, mountain of; Turning Point Academy)
    entertainment strategy of, 129
    financial statuses of, 19
    founding of, 5–6
    Frontlines, investigation team of, 77–79, 122–23
    gender events by, 85–89
    on LGBTQ matters, 79–80
    on masculinity, 83–84
    memes and, 136–37, 139
    mission statements of, 56–57
    pastoral training and, 62–64
    political impact of, 18–20
    pop culture and, 131–34
    racial-division markets of, 110–12
    racism and, 106–9
    as secular, 17–18
    sports and, 129–31
    Trump campaign and, 52, 111
    violence and, 40, 52–53
    watchlists of, 21–22, 35, 39–40
    See also Kirk, Charlie
Turning Point Academy, 19, 31, 36–39
Turning Point Action, 19, 136

Turning Point Faith, 19, 54
tyranny, 46, 50–53

universities. *See* higher education

Van Impe, Jack, 113–17
victim mentality, 106–9
violence, 3–4, 40, 50–53. *See also* Capitol insurrection
Violent Take It by Force, The (Taylor), 64
visions, from God, 1–2
voting rights, 44–45, 95–96
vouchers, school, 25, 35–37

Waco compound raid, 52–53
Wagner, C. Peter
    apostolic leadership and, 65–66, 103–4
    as charismatic, 16
    on Christian leadership, 70
    on cultural mandate, 14–15, 47
    on Islam, 73
    wealth and, 103–4, 106
Wallnau, Lance, 16–17, 62, 105, 120
Walton, Rus, 14
warfare
    culture, 61–62, 127–28, 133–34, 139–41
    spiritual, 8, 10, 15, 44–45, 47–48, 51–52, 61–62
warriors, of God, 83, 88
watchlists
    professor, 21–22, 39–40
    school boards, 35

wealth
    Christian, 16
    Christian culture advocates and, 10
    creation, 101
    divine role in, 97–98, 101–4
    great transfer of, 98–102, 109–11
    prophets and, 101–5
    victim mentality and, 106–9
Weber, Stu, 83
"White Boy Summer," 132–33
Wild at Heart (Eldredge), 84–85
Williams, Daniel K., 12
Wilson, Douglas, 37, 51
Winning God's Way (Cunningham), 46
Wolfe, William, 51, 58
women
    careers of, 89–90
    feminism and, 9, 82–83, 87
    fulfillment of, 88
    gender roles of, 80–82, 87–89, 91, 133
    as pop culture audience, 133–34
    as warriors of God, 83, 88
World Economic Forum, 124
worldview, biblical, 60–63

Young, Benjamin J., 8
Young Women's Leadership Summit, 87–89
youth, 8–9, 11, 41, 67–68, 88–89, 106
Youth with a Mission, 8–9, 11, 89, 106